Infamous Aircraft

Infamous Aircraft

Dangerous Designs and their Vices

Robert Jackson

Pen & Sword
AVIATION

First published in
Great Britain in 2005
By Pen and Sword Aviation
An imprint of
Pen and Sword Books Ltd
47 Church Street,
Barnsley,
South Yorkshire
S70 2AS

ISBN 1-84415-172-7

Typeset in 10/12pt Palatino
by Mac Style Ltd, Scarborough, N. Yorkshire

Printed and bound in Great Britain
by CPI UK

Pen and Sword Books Lieutenantd incorporates the imprints of Pen and
Sword Aviation, Pen and Sword Maritime, Pen and Sword Military,
Wharncliffe Local History, Pen and Sword Select, Pen and Sword
Military Classics and Leo Cooper.

For a complete list of Pen & Sword titles please contact
PEN & SWORD BOOKS LIMITED
47 Church Street, Barnsley, South Yorkshire, S70 2AS, England
E-mail: enquiries@pen-and-sword.co.uk
Website: www.pen-and-sword.co.uk

CONTENTS

CHAPTER ONE

Death Over the Trenches: the BE.2

The Albatros Scout cruised high over the front line, its young pilot eagerly scanning the drab, churned-up earth beneath, searching for the tell-tale flicker of movement that would betray the presence of an Allied reconnaissance aircraft. It had been several weeks since he had joined the famous *Jagdstaffel* 2 'Boelcke', and he had yet to score his first victory, a fact that caused him some frustration, surrounded as he was by some of Germany's top fighter pilots.

Now, on this morning of 27 November 1916, he was to have his chance at last. Just as he was about to go home, he sighted a British biplane, a couple of thousand feet lower down. Diving to the attack, he opened fire and saw his bullets ripping into the biplane's wings. The aircraft went down in a fast descent, its pilot apparently intent on getting down in one piece before the German shot him out of the sky. It crash-landed in no-man's land quite close to the British lines. The pilot and observer jumped from the cockpit and ran to the comparative safety of their own trenches. The German pilot circled overhead, raging. Since the biplane had come down outside German territory, there was no way of claiming it as a 'kill'; the German infantry who had occupied that particular sector had pulled out early that morning, and consequently there would be no witnesses.

Quickly, the young German decided on a drastic course of action. Throttling back, he glided down to land among the shell craters and came to a stop a few yards from the wreck of the British machine. Jumping down, he ran through the clinging mud and scrambled onto the biplane's splintered wing. He reached into the rear cockpit and pulled the machine-gun from its mounting. Burdened by his trophy, he stumbled back to his aircraft and threw himself into his seat, dragging the machine-gun with him. Mud sprayed up behind the wheels as he opened the throttle. Bullets crackled around him as the Albatros lurched into the air, but miraculously none struck home. That night, the machine-gun was mounted in the officers' mess of *Jagdstaffel* 2.

The German pilot was Leutnant Werner Voss, soon to become legendary as the 'Hussar of Krefeld', whose score of enemy aircraft destroyed would rise to forty-eight before his death in action in September 1917.

Voss's first victim, on that day in 1916, was a Royal Aircraft Factory BE.2c. It was an aircraft that was easy to fly; it had no vices; and it was inherently stable in flight. In combat, it was a death trap.

In 1909, HM Balloon Factory at Farnborough, which as its name implies had been involved in the production of lighter than air craft, began building aeroplanes. In 1912 the company changed its name to the Royal Aircraft Factory. Its first aircraft product, built in 1911, was the BE.1 (Blériot Experimental) tractor biplane, which was first flown on 1 January 1912. The pilot was 30-year-old Geoffrey de Havilland, who had joined the Balloon Factory in 1910. The rather curious Blériot Experimental designation was a smokescreen to cover up the fact that the aircraft had been designed by de Havilland and to give the impression that it was a repaired Blériot-type machine, for at that time the Balloon Factory was authorised to carry out repair work only.

The BE.1, which was built around a Wolseley engine, was quite an innovative design. It was followed by the BE.2, which used the same basic airframe and was the first military machine to be built as such in Britain. The BE.2 was one of the first successful attempts at building a fuselage biplane with a tractor engine driving a four-bladed propeller. The wings were of two-spar structure, supported by two pairs of struts on each side. The fuselage was rectangular in cross-section with curved top decking, the pilot and observer being seated in tandem. The elevator and rudder were of metal construction with fabric covering. The BE.2 was powered by a 70 hp air-cooled Renault engine and, like the BE.1, it was used to carry out a great deal of trials work. Four BE.2s were ordered by Vickers, and the Royal Aircraft Factory was authorised to build another five.

Much of the experimental work with the BE.1/BE.2 involved improving the type's stability, a characteristic that was to prove its

The BE.2a, also known as the 'Army Tractor Biplane', was Britain's first truly successful military aircraft design.

Achilles' heel; but this was something which, until the BE found itself in a combat situation, no one could have envisaged. The unit that pioneered the BE's entry into service with the Royal Flying Corps (RFC) was No. 2 Squadron, one of the RFC's first heavier-than-air units (No. 1 Squadron being equipped with balloons and airships at this time). The RFC pilots liked the BE, and No. 2 Squadron crews faced a stern test in January 1913, when they were ordered to deploy from their original base at Farnborough to Montrose, on the east coast of Scotland.

An official history of the RFC records:

> *Five of its officers did the journey in nine days, two of them in BEs and three in Maurice Farmans. They took off on the 17 February, and that evening Lieutenant C.A.H. Longcroft, having been compelled to land at Littlemore, near Oxford, spent the night in the local lunatic asylum. The next stop was Newcastle. Only two of them reached it in the day and these had had to land many times to ask the way. The directions they received were more suitable for land than air travellers, since 'turnings in the road and well-known public houses are not easy to recognize from the air'. By the 26 February they had all arrived at Montrose, and here a period of strenuous training began. By September they had advanced sufficiently to take part in the Irish Command manoeuvres, flying 400 miles each way to do so with no engine failures.*

When the RFC deployed four squadrons and sixty-four aircraft to France on 13 August 1914, a few days after the outbreak of war, two of them (Nos 2 and 4), were equipped entirely with BEs. By this time, new models of the basic design had made their appearance, production having given way to the BE.2a with wings of unequal span; the BE.2b with revised decking around the cockpits and ailerons instead of wing-warping controls; and the BE.2c.

The BE.2c, which appeared in the spring of 1914, differed radically from its predecessors. Its wings had greater stagger and dihedral, but the principal innovation was the addition of ailerons on all four wing sections. These changes further improved the stability of the aircraft, which was enhanced even more by a greatly increased rudder area. The undercarriage was also of a new design and much simpler, dispensing with skids. The wing tips were reshaped, becoming less rounded, and neat cut-outs at the trailing edge of the lower wing roots greatly improved downward visibility. The engine, designated RAF-1a, was a British version of the 70 hp Renault, with the output increased to 90 hp.

At the outbreak of the First World War, the principal version of the BE was the BE.2b.

The first wartime flight by a BE was made on Wednesday 19th August, when Lieutenant G.W. Mapplebeck of No. 4 Squadron took off from Maubeuge to make a reconnaissance of Gembloux, where enemy cavalry had been reported. He sighted a small group of them, and duly reported the fact back at his base.

Time after time, during the following weeks, the BE proved its worth in the air reconnaissance role. It had a longer range than most of the other types used at that time by the RFC, and consequently could penetrate deeper into enemy territory. On 15 September 1914, for the first time, the RFC made operational use of wireless telegraphy during artillery observation. Two BE.2s of No. 4 Squadron were involved. The pilots were Lieutenants D.S. Lewis and B.T. James, both of whom were later killed.

In March 1915 the British launched an offensive at Neuve Chapelle, an attack based – for the first time in history – on maps prepared solely from intelligence gathered by aerial photographic reconnaissance, much of it undertaken by BEs. As the assault got under way, the RFC launched the first tactical air bombing offensive, intended to delay the progress of enemy reinforcements.

Again, the BEs were in the thick of the fighting. Aircraft of Nos 4 and 6 Squadrons attacked the Menin junction and railway stations at Courtrai, Lille, Douai and Don, using 25 lb and 11 lb bombs. In April, BEs of Nos 2, 7 and 8 Squadrons also attacked railway stations during the battle for Ypres. It was during this battle that Lieutenant W.B. Rhodes-Moorhouse of No. 2 Squadron became the first RFC pilot to be awarded the Victoria Cross. Descending to low level to make sure of hitting a target on the line west of Courtrai railway station with his 100 lb bomb, he ran into heavy rifle and machine-gun fire. Despite being wounded three times, he regained his airfield at Merville, but succumbed to his wounds the next day.

The early part of 1915 saw massive strides in the development of the embryo science of air fighting. Right from the start of the conflict, it had been obvious that the machine-gun provided the best means of both attack and defence for the crew of an aircraft; this had already been demonstrated during trials in Britain, France and the United States in the years leading up to the outbreak of hostilities. There were several problems to be overcome, however, before the solution became a practical reality.

First, machine-guns could be fitted only to the sturdier of the types then in service; on other aircraft, the weight penalty was unacceptable. There was also the problem of aiming and firing any sort of gun, as the pilot and observer were surrounded by a considerable wing area, with its attendant struts and bracing wires, and seated either behind or in front of a large and vulnerable wooden propeller. Nevertheless, the RFC and RNAS (Royal Naval Air Service) quickly adopted the 27 lb American-designed Lewis gun as standard armament for their observation aircraft, particularly the 'pusher' types in which the observer, who sat in front of the pilot, had a large cone of fire upwards, downwards and on either side. In the beginning, the gun mounting was usually devised by the observer to suit himself. The French selected the Hotchkiss, which like the Lewis was air-cooled; a belt-fed weapon, it initially proved too inflexible for the observer to handle and so a drum feed was adopted. The Germans chose the lightweight Parabellum MG 14, a modification of the water-cooled Maxim; this also had a drum magazine.

The BE.2c was the first variant to be armed with a machine-gun, the primary reason being that in the early versions the observer had occupied the front cockpit, from which it would have been impossible to use such a weapon. The reconnaissance biplane now had at least some defence against the German scouts that were now

The BE.2c was the first of the BE series to be armed with a machine-gun.

becoming organised into efficient fighting units; but technology was about to come into play that would give the Germans almost total air superiority over the Western Front for months to come. The new development was the synchronised machine-gun.

'Synchronisation' meant, quite simply, relating the rate of fire of a machine-gun to the rate of revolution of a propeller, so that the bullets missed the advancing and retreating blades, enabling the gun to fire forwards through the propeller disc – which in turn meant that the whole aircraft could be used as an aiming platform. The device was perfected by Anthony Fokker, the Dutch designer who, having been turned down by the British and the French, was building aircraft for Germany. Fokker designed a simple engine-driven system of cams and pushrods that operated the trigger of a Parabellum machine-gun once during each revolution of the propeller; in effect, the propeller fired the gun. The mechanism was successfully demonstrated on a Fokker M5K monoplane. This aircraft was given the military designation E.I (E stood for

Eindecker or monoplane), and so became the first of the Fokker monoplane fighters.

The 'Fokker Scourge,' as it came to be known, began on 1 July 1915, when *Leutnant* Kurt Wintgens of *Feldflieger Abteilung* (Flying Section) 62, flying the Fokker M5K, shot down a French Morane monoplane. There was no doubt about this claim, but since the Morane fell inside French lines it was not upheld by the German High Command. Meanwhile, the production Fokker E.I had begun to reach the front-line German units in June. The small number of machines available, in the hands of pilots whose names would soon become legendary, began to make their presence felt. Foremost among them were *Leutnants* Max Immelmann and Oswald Boelcke, both of *Feldflieger Abteilung* 62. The definitive version of the Fokker Eindecker was the E.III, some of which were armed with twin Spandau machine-guns. *Abteilung* 62 rearmed with the new type at the end of 1915. The Fokker Eindecker was the first dedicated fighter aircraft to see operational service, and for months it made Allied reconnaissance flights into German territory virtual suicide missions.

Max Immelmann's chance to test the Fokker Eindecker in action came on 1 August 1915, when he took off with Boelcke to attack some BE.2cs, which were bombing the German airfield at Douai. The subsequent official report tells the story:

At 6 am on 1 August Leutnant *Immelmann took off in a Fokker fighting monoplane in order to drive away the numerous (about ten to twelve) enemy machines which were bombing Douai aerodrome. He succeeded in engaging three machines showing French markings [in fact they were British – author] in the area between Arras and Vitry. Heedless of the odds against him, he made an energetic and dashing attack on one of them at close quarters. Although this opponent strove to evade his onslaught by glides and turns and the other two enemy aircraft tried to assist the attacked airman by machine-gun fire,* Leutnant *Immelmann finally forced him to land westward of and close to Berbîeres after scoring several hits on vital parts of the machine. The inmate, an Englishman (instead of an observer he had taken with him a number of bombs, which he had already dropped) was severely wounded by two cross-shots in his left arm.* Leutnant *Immelmann immediately landed in the neighbourhood of the Englishman, took him prisoner and arranged for his transport to the Field Hospital of the 1st Bavarian Reserve Corps. The machine was taken over by the* Abteilung. *There was no machine-gun on board. A sighting device for bomb-dropping has been removed and will be tested.*

Immelmann's second BE, and his third aerial victory, was encountered on 1 September 1915, his birthday. He was circling over Neuville village, acting as escort to a German artillery-spotting aircraft, when he sighted the British machine, which he erroneously described as a:

... Bristol biplane which is heading straight towards me. We are still 400 metres apart. Now I fly towards him; I am about 10–12 metres above him. And so I streak past him, for each of us has a speed of 120 kilometres an hour. After passing him I go into a turn. When I am round again, I find he has not yet completed his turning movement. He is shooting fiercely from his rear. I attack him in the flank, but he escapes from my sights for a while by a skilful turn. Several seconds later I have him in my sights once more. I open fire at 100 metres, and approach carefully. But when I am only 50 metres away, I have difficulties with my gun. I must cease fire for a time.

Meanwhile I hear the rattle of the enemy's machine-gun and see plainly that he has to change a drum after every 50 rounds. By this time I am up to within 30 or 40 metres of him and have the enemy machine well within my sights. Aiming carefully, I give him about another 200 rounds from close quarters, and then my gun is silent again. One glance shows me I have no more ammunition left. I turn away in annoyance, for now I am defenceless. The other machine flies off westward, i.e. homeward.

I am just putting my machine into an eastward direction, so that I can go home too, when the idea occurs to me to fly a round of the battlefield first, for otherwise my opponent might think he had hit me. There are three bullets in my machine. I look round for my 'comrade of the fray', but he is no longer to be seen. I am still 2500 metres up, so that we have dropped 600 in the course of our crazy turns.

At last I discover the enemy. He is about 1000 metres below me. He is falling earthward like a dead leaf. He gives the impression of a crow with a lame wing. Sometimes he flies a bit and then he falls a bit. So he has got a dose after all.

Now I also drop down and continue to watch my opponent. It seems as if he wants to land. And now I see plainly that he is falling. A thick cloud rises from the spot where he crashes, and then bright flames break out of the machine. Soldiers hasten to the scene. Now I catch my first glimpse of the biplane I intended to protect. It is going to land. So I likewise decide to land, and come down close to the burning machine. I find soldiers attending to one of the inmates.

He tells me that he is the observer. He is an Englishman. When I ask him where the pilot is, he points to the burning machine. I look, and he is right, for the pilot lies under the wreckage – burnt to a cinder. The observer is taken off to hospital ...

Immelmann's description admirably sums up the weakness and the strength of the BE.2 in combat. First, Immelmann easily completes his turn before the BE pilot is anywhere near completing his, enabling him to latch on to the British aircraft's tail and press home his attack; and second, the BE displays its inbuilt stability after the pilot, as Immelmann learns later, is shot through the neck and killed. The aircraft goes out of control, but literally rights itself and resumes level flight before departing again. This process happened several times before it hit the ground and the observer, who lived to tell the story, was thrown clear.

By the autumn of 1915, the losses suffered by the BEs and other reconnaissance aircraft at the hands of the Fokkers had risen to such an alarming degree that the RFC decreed that all reconnaissance sorties must be escorted. The immediate solution, though not a good one, was for one BE to act as the escort while the other took its photographs. This tactic ended too often in both BEs being destroyed. What was needed was a dedicated fighter aircraft.

The French rose to the challenge first with the introduction of the single-seat Nieuport 11 biplane, which was deployed in the late summer of 1915, albeit in small numbers. Nicknamed 'Baby' because of its diminutive size, it had a machine-gun mounted on the upper wing, enabling the pilot to fire forwards over the arc of the propeller. The Nieuport 11 also served with the RFC and the RNAS and was built under licence in Italy, where it remained the standard fighter type until 1917.

The Nieuport 11 virtually held the line against the Fokker Eindecker until the introduction of two British fighter types, the FE.2b and DH.2. The original FE.2a was completed in August 1913, but it was a year before the first twelve aircraft were ordered, the first of these flying in January 1915. Had matters moved more quickly, and production of the FE.2 been given priority, it is possible that the Fokker Eindecker would never have achieved the supremacy that it did. The first FE.2b flew in March 1915. In May a few production examples arrived in France for service with No. 6 Squadron RFC at Abeele, Belgium, but it was not until January 1916 that the first squadron to be fully equipped with the FE, No. 20, deployed to France. The FE.2b was a two-seat 'pusher' type aircraft, powered by a 120-hp Beardmore engine and armed with one Lewis gun in the front cockpit and a second on a telescopic mounting firing upwards over the wing centre-section. It was slightly slower than the Fokker E.III but a match for it in manoeuvrability. Later in the war the FE was used in the light night-bombing role. The FE.2d was a variant with a longer span. FE.2 production totalled 2325 aircraft.

The first dedicated RFC fighter squadron to deploy to France was No. 20, equipped with FE.2bs. It was followed, on 8 February 1916, by No. 24 squadron, armed with Airco (Aircraft Manufacturing Company) DH.2s. Designed by Geoffrey de Havilland, the DH.2 was a single-seat 'pusher' type, whose prototype had been sent to France in July 1915 for operational trials; unfortunately, it was brought down in enemy territory on 9 August. The DH.2 was powered by a 100 hp Monosoupape engine and was armed with a single Lewis gun mounted on a pivot in the prow, enabling it to be traversed from left to right or elevated upward and downward. In practice, pilots found this arrangement too wobbly and secured the gun in a fixed forward-firing position, using the whole aircraft as an aiming platform. Rugged and highly manoeuvrable, the DH.2 was to achieve more success in action against the Fokkers than any other Allied fighter type. No. 24 Squadron was commanded by Major L.G. Hawker, who on 25 July 1915, while flying a Bristol Scout of No. 5 Squadron, had been awarded the Victoria Cross for engaging three enemy aircraft in quick succession and shooting one down. It soon became one of the best-known Allied air units. It gained its first victory on 2 April 1916 and claimed its first Fokker on the 25th of that month. From then on its tally rose steadily. In June 1916 its pilots destroyed seventeen enemy aircraft, followed by twenty-three in July, fifteen in August, fifteen in September and ten in November. On 23 November, however, Major Hawker was shot down by an up-and-coming German pilot named Manfred von Richthofen. Some 400 DH.2s were built, many being shipped to the Middle East after they became obsolete on the Western Front.

The BE.2 was to have been replaced in first-line service during 1916 by another product of the Royal Aircraft Factory, the RE.8. Nicknamed 'Harry Tate' after the Cockney comedian, the RE.8 reconnaissance and artillery spotting aircraft resembled a scaled-up BE.2, but it had a much sturdier fuselage and far better armament. The first aircraft were delivered in the autumn of 1916 but were grounded after a series of accidents that led to the redesign of the tail unit. The RE.8 was subsequently very widely used, equipping thirty-three RFC squadrons. Like the BE.2, it was far too stable to be agile in combat and suffered serious losses, usually having to operate under heavy escort. It was not until the beginning of 1917

The FE.8, seen here in service with No. 41 Squadron, was one of the types developed to combat the Fokker menace.

that the RFC's reconnaissance squadrons in France began to receive a really viable aircraft, the Armstrong Whitworth FK.8. Designed by the talented Dutchman Frederick Koolhoven, who joined Armstrong Whitworth of Coventry in 1914, the FK.8 army co-operation aircraft – known to its crews as the 'Big AW' or 'Big Ack' – first flew in May 1916 and eventually equipped nine RFC squadrons at home and overseas. About 1400 were built in total, serving in the reconnaissance, patrol, day and night-bombing and ground-attack roles throughout 1917 and 1918. The FK.8 was well liked by its crews, partly for its excellent flying qualities and partly because of its ability to absorb a great deal of battle damage.

Two more variants of the BE.2, the 2d and 2e, appeared before production ceased late in 1916. The type ended its combat career with the RFC's home defence squadrons, where it enjoyed considerable success against German airships.

CHAPTER TWO

Sopwith Camel: the Two-edged Sword

During the fierce air fighting that characterised the last two years of the First World War, the Sopwith Camel destroyed more enemy aircraft than any other Allied fighter. To those pilots who mastered its vicious idiosyncracies, and turned them to their own advantage, it was a magnificent fighting machine; to those who did not, it was a potential killer.

The little biplane that became known as the Camel was designed by the Sopwith company as a successor to their graceful Pup and elegant Triplane. Armed with two fixed Vickers machine-guns and powered by a Clerget rotary engine, the new fighter was designated Sopwith F.1, the prototype emerging a few days before Christmas 1916. It was not a pretty aircraft; the adjectives stocky, pugnacious, stumpy and purposeful all fitted it perfectly.

The first thing that struck people was its compact nature. The Clerget engine was on an overhung mounting and was fitted with a circular cowling. The oil tank was situated immediately behind the engine back-plate and the guns were mounted above, their twin muzzles level with the front of the engine cowling. The cockpit was situated as far forward as possible, the pilot's feet virtually under the carburettor, his face close to the butts of the machine-guns. He sat in a wicker seat, immediately behind which was the main fuel tank. Each mainplane had two main spars, and the profiles of all flight surfaces were formed of steel tubing. The lower wing had a pronounced dihedral angle of five degrees, which contrasted sharply with the lack of dihedral on the upper wing. Ailerons were fitted to both upper and lower wing surfaces. With the emergence of the first prototype, one flaw became immediately apparent; the aircraft had been built with no central cut-out in the centre section of the upper wing, which meant that the pilot was blind in a steep turn. A central cut-out was built into the second and subsequent machines.

The breech mechanisms of the twin Vickers guns were covered by a high forward decking. On the first prototype, this sloped upwards to the forward edge of the cockpit, forming a kind of windscreen. This gave the forward fuselage of the F.1 a humped appearance which, so the story goes, is how the aircraft came to be called the Camel. This name was never adopted officially, the aircraft continuing to bear the official designation Sopwith Biplane F.1. Subsequent aircraft had a horizontal decking, and were fitted with a small transparent windscreen.

Early production aircraft were powered either by the 130 hp Clerget 9B or the 150 hp Bentley BR1 rotary engine, but later aircraft

Despite its often treacherous flying characteristics, the Sopwith Camel became the 'Spitfire' of the 1914–18 air war.

were fitted with either the Clerget or the 110 hp Le Rhone 9J. The rotary engine was attractive for fighters because it had a very good power/weight ratio – much better than an equivalent stationary engine – and it was very compact. Probably the best of them all was the Bentley BR2, which came along at the end of 1917. The excellent power/weight ratio was a by-product of the circumferential layout of the cylinders, which saved a lot of crankcase weight, and from the fact that the cooling was provided by the cylinders whirling round in the air stream. This permitted a very light steel cylinder, with minimum cooling fins.

In the air, however, having the main engine mass whirling round at about 1250 rpm introduced some peculiarities not apparent in stationary-engined aircraft. Of these, the most obvious was gyroscopic action. There was also a considerable increase in torque reaction, which tried to rotate the airframe in the opposite direction to the rotation of the engine. As one former Sopwith Camel pilot put it:

Some people, particularly learner pilots on Camels, regarded this mysterious gyroscopic action – it was very fierce on Camels – as a species of black magic malevolently exercised by a venomous aircraft to imperil the safety of its pilot; but if one took the trouble to understand it, this bogey of personal malevolence faded out and was replaced by a comforting knowledge of what was going on and what had to be done about it.

A gyroscope is any sort of spinning mass – like an ordinary spinning top – and the whirling mass of some 350 lb of engine at 1250 rpm constitutes a gyroscope of quite sizeable proportions. The outstanding feature of a gyroscope is that it likes to stay in the geometric plane in which it is spinning. If the axis of rotation is turned, as in turning the aeroplane, the gyroscope, following its urge to stay put, registers a strong protest by tilting on an axis at right-angles to the desired axis of turn. In terms of practical flying this means that if, with an engine rotating clockwise as seen from the pilot's seat, you turn to the right, the gyroscopic effect will give a sharp nose-down reaction; or, if you turn to the left, it will give a nose-up effect. Similarly, a sudden climb produces a strong swing to the right and a dive produces a swing to the left. These effects are, of course, present in a small degree on any propeller-driven aircraft, but in some of the rotaries they were really fierce.

In the Camel, the engine, guns, pilot and fuel were all concentrated at the front end of the fuselage, which made response to rudder and elevators very lively. It also made response to the queer effects of gyroscopic action very lively, too. So much was this so, with the heavier engine, that gyroscopic effect became quite a problem and on sudden changes of direction the Camel could, and with unwary pilots often did, run out of rudder control – sometimes with disastrous results. To this rather daunting characteristic was added an unusual readiness to spin, presumably a side effect of the compact concentration of weight.

In his book *Recollections of an Airman*, Lieutenant-Colonel L.A. Strange, an experienced Camel pilot who served with the Central Flying School at Upavon, Wiltshire, from April 1917 to March 1918, wrote:

> *In spite of all the care we took, Camels continually spun down out of control when flown by pupils on their first solos. At length, with the assistance of Lieut Morgan, who managed our workshops, I took the main tank out of several Camels and replaced it with a smaller one, which enabled us to fit in dual control. When the first of these adapted machines was ready, Morgan was my passenger on its first flight.*

In the hands of a skilled pilot, who was able to use its vicious engine torque to his own advantage, the Camel was deadly.

Two-seat Camel conversions were also made at other flying establishments, and dual instruction went some way to alleviating the unacceptable casualty problem during the critical training phase.

The first unit to receive Camels was No. 4 Squadron RNAS, followed by No. 70 Squadron RFC, both in July 1917. By the end of the year 1325 Camels (out of a total of 3450 on order at that time) had been delivered, and were used widely for ground attack during the Battles of Ypres and Cambrai. In March 1917, meanwhile, a shipboard version of the Camel, the 2F.1, had undergone trials; designed to operate from platforms on warships, from towed lighters or from the Royal Navy's new aircraft carriers, this differed from the F.1 in having a slightly shorter wing span. Also, instead of the starboard Vickers gun, it had a Lewis gun angled to fire upwards through a cutout in the upper wing centre section. The 2F.1's principal mission was Zeppelin interception; 340 examples were built, but the first of these did not become operational until the spring of 1918. By the end of the war, however, 2F.1 Camels were deployed on five aircraft carriers, two battleships and twenty-six cruisers of the Royal Navy. On 11 August 1918, a 2F.1 Camel flown by Lieutenant Stuart Culley, and launched from a lighter towed behind the destroyer HMS *Redoubt*, intercepted and destroyed the Zeppelin L.53 over the Heligoland Bight.

Early in 1918, with an increase in night attacks on southern England by German heavier-than-air bombers, several home-based night-fighter units rearmed with the Sopwith Camel. The cessation of night attacks in May meant that aircraft could be released for service in the night-fighting role on the Western Front. In June, No. 151 Squadron, a specialist Camel-equipped night-fighting unit, moved to France and began operations against Gotha night bombers and their airfields.

At the end of October 1918 the RAF had 2548 Camel F.1s on charge, and 129 2F.1s. By this time the Camel was already being replaced by the Sopwith Snipe, but it continued to serve for some years after the war with the Belgian *Aviation Militaire*, the Canadian Air Force, the Royal Hellenic Naval Air Service, the Polish Air Force and the US Navy.

The last RAF squadron to use the Camel in combat was No. 47, which deployed to southern Russia in March 1919 to support the Allied Intervention Force, in action against the Bolsheviks. During the same period, Camels operating from the carrier HMS *Vindictive* flew in support of Allied forces resisting Russian advances into the Baltic States.

The Camel's fighting prowess is well illustrated by a few accounts of its actions on the Western Front in 1918, when it really came into its own. The following is an extract from the war diary of No. 43 Squadron, then based at La Gorgue under the command of Major C.C. Miles.

17 February. Trollope's patrol of five Camels encountered an enemy formation of eight machines. As a result of the combat which ensued three enemy machines were driven down out of control.

18 February. Captain Trollope while on a special mission (alone) saw three Armstrong Whitworths under attack by six enemy machines. He at once attacked the enemy who were then joined by six more. Trollope fought the twelve for ten minutes until all his ammunition was exhausted, by which time the enemy machines had all flown away to the east.

19 February. Second Lieutenant R.J. Owen whilst on patrol on his own was attacked by five enemy scouts in the vicinity of the Bois de Biez. He fought the five, one of which according to the testimony of anti-aircraft gunners was seen to fall in flames.

26 February. Captain Trollope leading a patrol of nine Camels saw four DFWs escorted by fifteen enemy scouts. He led the patrol into the attack. Although gun trouble prevented him from joining in he stayed in the middle of the fight and saw two enemy machines crash and a third fall out of control.

At the beginning of March 1918, there were plenty of indications that an expected German offensive in Flanders was not far away. Despite continuing bad weather the enemy's air effort intensified, with much activity by observation aircraft. There were some brisk engagements, and on 13 March seven Camels of No. 43 Squadron, escorting a pair of FK.8s, encountered a mixed force of fifteen Albatros and Pfalz scouts and attacked them; Captain Henry Woollett fired at one, which broke up in mid-air, then engaged a second, which went out of control and crashed. Two more were shot down by 2nd Lieutenant Peiler, and one each by 2nd Lieutenants Lingham, Lomax, King and Dean. A ninth enemy aircraft was shot down by an observer in one of the FK.8s, which belonged to No. 2 Squadron, whereupon the remainder broke off the action and flew away.

On 16 March, seven Camels of No. 4 (Australian) Squadron, which was part of the 10th (Army) Wing, took off from Bruay to attack targets near Douai with 20 lb bombs. The attack was carried out without incident, but as the Camels were climbing to 16,000 feet to cross the front line they were hotly engaged by a formation of sixteen brightly painted Albatros scouts, readily identifiable as belonging to the Richthofen *Geschwader*. While four of the Albatros remained at altitude, ready to dive down and pick off stragglers, the other twelve attacked in pairs. The Australian flight commander, Lieutenant G.F. Malley and Lieutenant C.M. Feez avoided the first pass and went in pursuit of the two Albatros, which were diving in formation. The Australians shot both of them down. Meanwhile, Lieutenant A.W. Adams, some 2000 feet lower down, fought a hectic battle with two more Scouts and destroyed one of them, while Lieutenant W.H. Nicholls, pursued down to ground level, was forced to land behind the German lines and was taken prisoner. Another Camel pilot, Lieutenant P.K. Schafer, was attacked by three Albatros of the high flight; as he was attempting to evade, the Camel flicked into a spin and fell 10,000 feet before the shaken Australian managed to recover. He landed at Bruay with sixty-two bullet holes in his aircraft. On the following day, Captain John Trollope of No. 43 Squadron sighted six enemy Scouts while flying alone on an altitude test (a favourite ploy of pilots lacking the necessary authorisation to carry out lone patrols over the front line). He climbed above them and attacked, sending one down out of control. The other five dived away. Shortly afterwards, while returning to base, Trollope sighted four more enemy aircraft and attacked one of them at close range. It caught fire and broke up. Trollope at once turned to engage the rest, but they flew away eastwards.

The big German offensive was launched on 21 March 1918. Some fighter squadrons, which had been operating from bases outside the immediate battle area, were now moved closer to it in order to provide escort for the all-important ground attack and observation aircraft, and to establish the air superiority that was so vital to the RFC's effort. One of them was No. 43 Squadron, which moved from La Gorgue, near Merville, to Avesnes-le-Comte near Arras. On the first patrol on 24 March, Captain John Trollope, leading a flight of Camels, sighted three DFW two-seaters and worked his way round to the east to cut off their line of escape. He closed in and fired at the first, but then his guns jammed. After clearing the stoppage he engaged the second DFW and fired 100 rounds at it, seeing it break up in mid-air; he at once closed on a third and set it on fire. Meanwhile, the first DFW had been engaged by Captain Cecil King and 2nd Lieutenant A.P. Owen, who continued to fire at it until it too broke up. Some Albatros scouts arrived belatedly to protect the D.F.W.s, and Trollope immediately shot one down. At a lower level,

A German pilot falls clear of his blazing Albatros scout. This was the result of many an encounter with a Sopwith Camel.

another flight of No. 43 Squadron Camels led by Captain Henry Woollett was engaging more D.F.Ws, one of which Woollett set on fire. Lieutenant Daniel of Woollet's flight, losing contact during the engagement, joined up with No. 3 (Naval) Squadron, which attacked five Pfalz scouts. Daniel destroyed one of them, bringing No. 43 Squadron's score on that patrol to six.

That afternoon, Trollope led a second patrol into action, despite deteriorating weather conditions. Soon after crossing the front line he sighted four enemy two-seaters attacking a pair of RE.8s; five or six German single-seat fighters were also in the vicinity. Trollope led his pilots down to the aid of the REs and he singled out one of the two-seaters, firing in short bursts as he closed in to almost point-blank range. He saw pieces fly off the enemy aircraft's wing, and then the whole wing collapsed. Turning hard, Trollope came round for a stern attack on another two-seater, running through heavy defensive fire from the German observer as he did so. A few moments later the German was dead in his cockpit and the aircraft spiralling down in flames. Almost at once, Trollope engaged a third two-seater which was flying at very low level; after a short burst of fire the enemy aircraft nose-dived into the ground, disintegrating on impact.

Pulling up, Trollope saw one of the squadron's Camels hard-pressed by a dozen German scouts, so he climbed hard to assist, soon joined by 2nd Lieutenants Owen and Highton. He saw each of these pilots destroy an enemy aircraft and engaged one himself, but then his ammunition ran out and he was forced to break off. In the afternoon, nine Camels led by Captain Henry Woollett fired 6800 rounds in strafing attacks on enemy troops, and Woollett also shot down two observation balloons. By the end of the day, Lieutenant 'Bert' Hull, No. 43 Squadron's records officer, could report to his CO, Major Miles, that the unit had broken all previous records, having destroyed twenty-two enemy aircraft without loss in the day's fighting. The destruction of six by Captain Trollope in a single day had created a new RFC/RNAS record. There could have been no finer vindication for the aircraft they called a killer.

CHAPTER THREE

Death of a Giant:
the Airship R.101

In 1924, the British Government initiated an airship research programme, its purpose being to establish whether large rigid airships would be commercially viable. The programme, which was to be spread over three years at a cost of £1,350,000, was to lead to the construction of two experimental airships capable of carrying a large payload on intercontinental flights. The ships, designated R.100 and R.101, were to be built respectively by the Airship Guarantee Company – a subsidiary of Vickers – and the Air Ministry establishment at Cardington, Bedfordshire. The Air Ministry was also to construct airship bases in Egypt, Canada and India.

The civilian Airship Guarantee Company was hampered from the start by a shortage of money, but the lack of funds was more than compensated for by the genius of the men in control of the enterprise. The chief designer was Dr Barnes Wallis – a man of great talent and revolutionary ideas, with a vast amount of design experience on earlier Vickers rigid airships. His work in this field was to be overshadowed by later fame in connection with the bombs that smashed the Möhne and Eder dams in 1943. His chief calculator was a young man who was also to earn fame, but in a different sphere: Nevil Shute Norway.

The specifications that governed the development of both the R.100 and R.101 were stringent. Both ships were to have a capacity of five million cubic feet, giving them a gross lift of 150 tons, and their structure had to meet certain definite stress factors. The maximum speed with 100 passengers on board was to be not less than 70 mph, with a cruising speed of 63 mph. The structural weight, including the power plants but excluding fuel, was not to exceed 90 tons, giving a useful lift of 60 tons. The engines and their fuel systems were to be capable of operating efficiently in tropical climates.

The Air Ministry designers of the R.101 at Cardington had to start virtually from scratch; the only airship design they could take as a guide was that of an earlier rigid craft, the R.38. This airship had broken up in flight over the river Humber in August 1921 with heavy loss of life. The problem was that no stress calculations on the R.38's structure existed, so the Cardington team's first task was to carry out a thorough investigation into the aerodynamic forces acting on an airship in flight, and to compile data on the distribution of stresses in the structure of an airship caused by those aerodynamic forces and by static forces resulting from loading and other factors.

The basic research work was undertaken by the scientists of the National Physical Laboratory, who tested various models in wind tunnels to evolve a definite shape that would cut down air resistance to the absolute minimum. To check out the data compiled with the aid of these models, two rigid airships that had been laid up for some time, the R.33 and R.36, were recommissioned and their hulls and control surfaces festooned with instruments for measuring stresses and strains. A complete hull section of the R.101 was also built at Cardington and tested to destruction. The designers professed the results to be satisfactory, but there is no doubt that they stopped at a crucial point in the R.101's development. The airship's construction was an almost complete breakaway from conventional methods, from the gasbag wiring and the relief valves right down to the steering gear and the type of engine to be used. However, just when the R.33 and R.36 could have been used profitably to test these new techniques under actual flight conditions, the government ordered the scrapping of both airships on grounds of economy.

The first step had therefore been taken on the road that was to lead to disaster. Although many problems were solved by means of theoretical calculations made with the use of models, this was no substitute for full-scale flight testing. Although the information gathered by the Air Ministry team was made available to the Airship Guarantee Company, there was no real cooperation between the two. Approaches made by Barnes Wallis and his colleagues with a view to closer collaboration were ignored, despite the fact that relations remained quite friendly. Throughout the period of construction, the Cardington team received an enormous amount of publicity. This in itself was another contributory factor to the eventual tragedy. As each new technique and refinement in the R.101's design came along, it received so much publicity that the designers felt compelled to incorporate it, even if it showed poor results during trials.

One good example of this was the R.101's specially developed diesel engines. The decision to use diesels had been influenced by safety considerations, diesel fuel burning less fiercely than petrol. The snag was that the engines were far too heavy, with a weight of eight pounds per horsepower instead of the estimated four. Moreover, no amount of modification would coax the engines to develop more than 650 hp each – and the requirement had specified a minimum of 700 hp.

Diesels of the R.101 type had also been considered as a possible power source for the R.100, but the fact that they were too heavy was discovered in time and they were replaced by six Rolls-Royce Condor petrol engines. The risk of fire from these motors was only marginally greater than if diesels were used, and the Condors had an overwhelming advantage in that they were already tried and proven. In general, the constructors of the R.100 went about their task in a much more workmanlike fashion, detecting snags and eliminating them in the early stages before much money had been wasted. Construction went ahead steadily with none of the fuss and

The R.101 at her Cardington mooring mast. The airship was a disaster from start to finish.

publicity that surrounded the R.101. In the middle of 1929 the ship's fourteen gasbags were inflated and she was floated in her shed, still without her outer envelope.

The R.101 was completed first. On 12 October 1929 she was walked out of her shed and moored at the Cardington mast in readiness for her maiden flight, which took place on the 14th. It lasted five and a half hours and for most of the time only two of her five troublesome engines were working, but on her second flight – made on 18 October and lasting nine and a half hours – four engines were in operation. Incredibly, no written reports on either of these flights were made. The third test flight was made on 1 November and lasted seven and a half hours. The following day the airship made her first night flight, taking off from Cardington at 20.00 hours and setting course towards the Isle of Wight. During this flight the ship was scheduled to make a speed trial, but one of her engines broke down and the attempt had to be abandoned. The R.101 finally landed back at Cardington at 10.00 hours on 3 November.

A week later, on 11 November, a severe gale blew up while the R.101 was at her mooring mast. Throughout most of the afternoon the average wind speed was 55 mph, and gusts of up to 83 mph were recorded. The ship rode out the gale successfully, withstanding a load of over 15 tons on her nose coupling, but she experienced a slow rolling motion during the stronger gusts of wind and her gasbags became chafed and punctured through contact with metal struts.

The damage was repaired, and on 17 November the R.101 set off on an endurance flight that was to have lasted 48 hours. In fact, the flight was abandoned because of various technical troubles after 30 hours 41 minutes, but during this time the ship covered a distance of 1000 miles. It was the longest flight she was ever to make. Afterwards, the ship remained at her mooring mast until 30 November, when she was taken into her shed. So far, she had made a total of seven flights and logged 70 hours in the air, but all the flights had been made in good weather and none had involved a lengthy full-speed trial.

Meanwhile, in November 1929, the R.100 had also made her maiden flight. In December she was flown from Howden in Yorkshire, where she had been built, and moored at Cardington for the start of her trials. She soon showed herself to be much the better of the two ships, clocking a speed of 81 mph during her early trials flights and showing herself capable of operating in all weathers.

Her design was somewhat unusual, with tubular longitudinal girders and a passenger coach built inside the hull instead of protruding beneath, as was more common.

Although the R.100 suffered a number of technical troubles with her envelope and gasbags, her performance met the specification quite adequately. The success of her test-flight programme did nothing to raise the morale of the R.101 team, especially since the effects of the American depression were making themselves felt in Britain's economy and there was a strong rumour that the less successful of the two airships would be scrapped. A prestige flight to India was in the wind, but before there was the remotest chance of this taking place something had to be done to increase the R.101's useful lift. At only 25 tons it was less than half that of the R.100. After lengthy discussions, the designers decided to remove some of the ship's fittings, including some of the passenger sleeping accommodation, and to enlarge the gasbag wiring to allow greater expansion. This, it was estimated, would increase the useful lift by about 6 tons. Another 9 tons could be obtained by creating an additional middle bay, allowing space for another gasbag by lengthening the ship.

Even with these modifications, the flight to India could still not be attempted until the airship had received a full Certificate of Airworthiness, and one of the requirements for this was an endurance flight of at least 48 hours. Accordingly, it was decided to complete the first set of modifications and then put the R.101 through a further series of test flights before adding the new bay and gasbag.

When the airship was examined prior to the rewiring of the gasbags, it was found that every one of the bags was holed, some of them badly. No. 11 bag, for example, had 103 holes and No. 5 had 57. These were repaired, and the projections thought to be responsible for the damage were carefully padded. The designers realised that enlarging the bags was going to add to the danger, but the plan went ahead. Their solution to the problem was simply to increase the amount of padding. The complex and weighty servo-controls governing elevators and rudder were also scrapped and replaced with a simpler and lighter control system similar to that installed in the R.100.

It was six months before these modifications were completed, and it was not until 23 June 1930 that the R.101 emerged from her shed once more. She had hardly been manoeuvred into position at her mooring mast when, without warning, a split 140 feet long appeared in the starboard side of her envelope. This was quickly repaired, but the next day a smaller split appeared in the top of the envelope. Both crew and designers knew that if the envelope ripped open in such a manner while the ship was airborne, the consequences would be catastrophic. Nevertheless, the test programme went ahead with a four-and-a-half-hour flight on 26 June. During this trip, the ship's eighth, the craft became dangerously heavy through loss of lift and over 2 tons of diesel fuel had to be jettisoned before a safe landing could be made.

As part of a renewed publicity programme, the R.101 was scheduled to take part in the RAF air pageant at Hendon. On 27 June she took off on a rehearsal flight that lasted twelve and a half hours. To keep her at an altitude of 1000 feet the crew had to jettison 9 tons of water ballast. The airship flew over Hendon the following day and the trouble was repeated, the craft losing height steadily as she leaked large quantities of gas. The crowd that watched her as she cruised overhead and marvelled at her majesty never dreamed that she was virtually crippled, and that her crew had to use all their skill to bring her safely back to Cardington.

On 29 June the R.101 was taken back into her shed so that work could begin on inserting the new bay. Once more, she was subjected to a thorough overhaul, which revealed a number of horrifying faults. First, it was found that when the valves on the gas cells were tilted at an angle of four degrees or more from the vertical, they opened. This meant that gas was bound to escape at a fast rate if the ship rolled beyond the four-degree limit as she passed through areas of turbulence. Second it was discovered that the padding around the gas cells had proved inadequate. The bags were now being fouled by literally thousands of projections. There were two possible solutions: a drastic alteration of the structure, or more padding. Predictably, it was the latter alternative that was chosen.

Meanwhile, the R.100 had completed seven test flights, most of them successful, and had logged a total of 150 hours in the air. She was now ready for the first of the 'Empire' flights, which, it was hoped, she would eventually share with the R.101, and on 29 July 1930 she left her mooring mast at Cardington bound for Montreal. Despite running through heavy storms after crossing the Atlantic, and suffering some repairable damage, she landed at Montreal on 1 August after a flight of 78 hours 51 minutes.

Departing on the eastbound crossing on 13 August, she reached Cardington on the 16th after an airborne time of 56 hours 30 minutes, having taken advantage of the prevailing wind.

Afterwards, she was taken back to her shed and overhauled in readiness for more flights abroad. But the R.100 never flew again. The tragedy that was about to befall the R.101 saw to that.

Work on the R.101 had been going on round the clock in a desperate attempt to make the ship ready for a flight to India in September. Despite all this effort, it was clear that the ship would not be ready before the end of September at the earliest, and the Cardington team were reluctant to take her on such a voyage before she was fully certificated – which meant a flight of 48 hours under normal conditions, one of 24 hours in adverse weather, and high-speed trials. The procedure was complicated still further by the Air Minister, Lord Thomson. He announced his intention to visit India in September to take part in a number of political engagements and saw no reason why the R.101 should not be ready in time to take him there. He had aspirations to become the next Viceroy of India, and wished to create as big an impression as possible by arriving in dramatic fashion. His views were expressed in a minute to the director of the Airship Works at Cardington. 'I must insist,' he wrote, 'on the programme for the Indian flight being adhered to as I have made my plans accordingly.' Those plans involved being back in England not later than 19 October, in order to participate in an Imperial Conference on the 20th.

When he learned that the ship would not be complete in time to make the flight in September, Thomson was furious. Nevertheless, he revised his schedule to allow for a departure on 4 October – but not a day later. The Cardington team stifled their protests: argument would have almost certainly meant the end of the R.101 project. Instead, they rushed the work on the new bay, leaving no time for real testing either on the ground or in flight. Hasty repairs were also carried out on the envelope, which was in a pitiful state, but there was no time to replace it entirely. Several parts were simply patched up with tape, attached to the doped fabric with a rubber solution – in complete ignorance of the fact that rubber solution and dope do not mix. The work was completed by 25 September, and over the next few days a number of lift and trim tests were carried out inside the R.101's shed. It was found that the extra bay now gave the ship a useful lift of 49.3 tons. On 1 October she was taken out of her shed and took off on a flight lasting 16 hours 51 minutes.

The flight took place in perfect weather conditions and it had been hoped to put the airship through her high-speed trials, but this plan was abandoned when one of the R.101's engines broke down.

The following day, Sir Sefton Brancker, the Director
Aviation, called on Lord Thomson and confided that h
from happy about the R.101's state of airworthiness. Wing
Commander Colmore, the Director of Airship Development, also
shared his views; both men wanted the R.101 put through more
trials before she was taken on a journey of such magnitude,
particularly one during which she would be subjected to enormous
variations in temperature as she passed over regions such as the
Alps and the Sahara. Thomson refused to listen. The R.101 was, he
declared, as safe as a house – except for the millionth chance.

The ship still had no Certificate of Airworthiness, and without
one the planned flight to India was illegal. But there was an answer
to this, too, even though it involved a slight bending of the
regulations. Shortly before the airship took off, a temporary
certificate was handed to her captain, Flight Lieutenant H.C. Irwin.
It was also decided that the qualifying full-speed trials would be
made during the voyage itself with all the passengers and crew on
board.

At 18.56 hours on 4 October 1930 the R.101's 777-foot length
slipped away from the Cardington mast and the journey to India
began. On board were fifty-four people – forty-two crew, six
officials from the Airship Works, and six passengers, including Lord
Thomson and Sir Sefton Brancker. The airship carried 25 tons of
fuel and $9^1/_4$ tons of water, but 4 tons of this were dropped while
the ship was still at her mast. The wind was blowing in gusts and
its strength increasing all the time. As the R.101 cruised over Hitchin
(Hetfordshire) at 1000 feet she encountered a rainstorm. As she
passed through it an alarming rolling and pitching motion
developed. Soon afterwards, the aft engine broke down. Two
engineers were detailed to repair it, and the ship continued on her
way.

At 21.35 hours the R.101 crossed the Channel coast at Hastings
and the captain sent a signal to Cardington reporting that although
the faulty engine was still out of action, the ship generally appeared
to be responding well. The engine was eventually restarted halfway
across the Channel, but by this time the ship was down to 700 feet,
and it was only with extreme difficulty that she was able to regain
1000 feet.

At 23.26 hours the airship crossed the French coast at Pointe-Saint-
Quentin, north-east of Dieppe. She was now making slow progress
against a headwind of 35 knots and experiencing severe buffeting
as she ran through areas of turbulence. Despite this, Flight

Lieutenant Irwin still seemed pleased with the ship's performance, as was indicated by another signal that he transmitted to Cardington: 'After an excellent supper our distinguished passengers smoked a final cigar and, having sighted the French coast, have now gone to rest after the excitement of the leave-taking.'

With all the passengers and most of the crew in bed, the duty crew settled down on watch in the control cabin. It seems certain that they had a continual struggle to maintain height, for when the airship passed over Poix airfield at 01.00 hours, observers on the ground estimated her altitude as no more than 300 feet. At 01.52 hours the ship radioed Le Bourget and gave her position as five-eighths of a mile north of Poix, her altimeter indicating 1000 feet above sea level. It was her last message.

At 02.00 hours the watch was changed. The ship was passing over Beauvais, and residents of the town who saw her stated later that she was rolling badly. She was very low. At 02.05 hours, without warning, the R.101 went into a steep dive, which was checked just in time by the release of water ballast. The coxswain fought to bring her nose up, but the elevators failed to respond; the ship was too heavy and too low. Seconds later she went into another, more shallow dive, and at 02.08 hours she struck a hillside near Beauvais with a prolonged crunching noise. The airship skidded along on her keel for sixty yards; the impact was quite gentle, and those on board who were fully awake prepared to make an emergency exit as soon as the motion stopped. But there was no time. An instant later, five and a half million cubic feet of hydrogen erupted and the R.101 became a blazing funeral pyre from stem to stern. Of the fifty-four on board there were six survivors, all of whom had miraculous escapes. Lord Thomson and Sir Sefton Brancker were not among them.

An inquiry concluded that part of the fabric on top of the airship's envelope had torn away during the buffeting she had received over the French coast. The gasbags, already badly chafed, would then have been further damaged by exposure to the weather and sprung leaks – and more gas must have been lost through the continual opening of the valves as the ship rolled, as this fault had never been rectified. The result was that she became steadily heavier and more waterlogged, until she became powerless to recover from the sudden downdraughts that seized her. She crashed to her destruction on the rain-swept hillside near Beauvais, a burnt-out testimony to bungling, mismanagement and crass governmental stupidity, which, fortunately, has had few parallels in the history of aviation.

The destruction of the R.101, and the death of many of the finest brains associated with airship development, marked the end of Britain's part in the story of the big rigids. The R.100 never flew again; she was broken up and sold as scrap for £450, an ignominious end to a good ship, and to the years of skill and devotion that had gone into her making.

CHAPTER FOUR

The Mignet Flying Flea: a Dream that Went Wrong

T he Mignet Flying Flea of the 1930s, which brought both triumph and tragedy to those aviation enthusiasts who built and flew it, was created because its designer, Henri Mignet, lacked the coordination of hands and feet necessary for him to learn to fly a conventional light aircraft. Desperate to learn to fly, Mignet put his agile brain to work on the dilemma, and came up with the notion of designing a simple, cheap sports aircraft in which some of the flying controls – the rudder bar, for example – were eliminated altogether.

Born in France in 1893, Henri Mignet displayed an early passion for aviation. In 1912, inspired by gliding pioneer Otto Lilienthal – whose articles on flying he had devoured avidly – he designed and built a monoplane glider, the HM-1-1. It was the first of several designs that he produced in subsequent years. None was successful, and his experiments were interrupted by the First World War, in which he served as a wireless telegraphist. In the mid-1920s, now married, he took up chicken farming. This not only supported his family, but also provided the necessary funding for further aviation research. In 1926 he designed the HM-6, a low-powered ultra-light aircraft with the engine situated behind the pilot. In this aircraft, instead of using a conventional elevator control to provide movement in the pitching (up-and-down) axis, he employed a wing that pivoted around its aerodynamic centre, so varying its angle of incidence. The aircraft was not a success, and although Mignet managed to get the HM-6's tail off the ground, the machine would not rise into the air.

Mignet used parts of the HM-6 in his next design, the HM-8 of 1928. Powered by a motorcycle engine, this design, which Mignet called the 'Avionette', flew successfully. It was tested over a two-month period, Mignet teaching himself to fly at the same time. There were frequent crashes, fortunately none of a serious nature; most of them involved only the replacement of the propeller. On 22 March 1928, Mignet published details of his little aircraft in the magazine *Wings* and generated immediate interest. This intensified when he published a book giving an account of how he had built the aircraft. It sold out in a week. Soon, Mignet's design – now named the Pou du Ciel, or Flying Flea – was being built by amateurs all over France. The first to take to the air, on 21 May 1929, was built by Jean Joubert of Angouleme.

The Flying Flea was simplicity itself. It had just one control lever which, if moved back and forth, swung the whole wing up and down about the main spar, and if the lever was moved from side to side, the rudder moved. The aircraft had two large wings, one behind the other in tandem, no tailplane, no elevators and no ailerons. Before long, news of the 'Flea craze' that was sweeping France reached England, where the little aircraft and its inventor quickly became news. British interest quickened when the *Daily Express*, already noted for its support of aviation, reported that a Flea was being built by an English enthusiast, Stephen Villiers Appleby, who had contacted Mignet and purchased a set of plans. The completed aircraft was allocated the registration G-ADMH and received Permit to Fly No. 1 on 14 July 1935. Just eleven days later, Appleby took off from Heston and came to grief, landing upside down in a field, fortunately without injury to himself. The *Daily Express* obligingly provided the money for the Flea to be rebuilt.

Appleby's Flea was rebuilt incorporating some design changes that were suggested by sailplane designer L. E. Baynes, who had seen the little aircraft crash at Heston. The wing was reconstructed using stronger spars, its span being lengthened by five feet, and the forward wing's pivotal point was moved further forward relative to the chord line.

Meanwhile, Henri Mignet had decided to subject his Pou du Ciel to its sternest test so far. On 12 August 1935, he flew to Calais on the first stage of a planned cross-Channel flight to England. However, the touchdown at Calais turned into one of Mignet's

This Flying Flea was restored (although not to flying condition) by members of an Air Training Corps squadron in the 1970s.

customary bad landings and he crashed, damaging the Flea's engine. Undeterred, he told airport officials that he intended to set off for England the next day, and went off in search of a replacement engine. The following afternoon, he turned up with a 22 hp Aubier et Dunne motor, installed it in the Flea, and made a short test flight, which went smoothly. Just after 7 pm on 13 August, he tied an inflated bicycle inner tube round his waist (as an insurance against having to 'ditch' his aircraft) and took off, heading into a strong north-easterly wind. Halfway across the Channel, he was met by an aircraft chartered by the *Daily Express*, which escorted him to Lympne, on the clifftops of the Kentish coast. He landed without mishap at 7.53 pm.

Sponsored by the *Daily Express*, Mignet spent the next few days touring the south coast seaside resorts. The Flea attracted huge interest. On 17 August, a crowd of 14,000 descended on the grass airfield at Shoreham to watch him put the tiny aircraft through its paces. Enthusiasm ran riot. Here, at last, was an aeroplane within the reach of everybody. It could be built in a garden shed for as little as £70, and its pilot needed no formal flying instruction; he could teach himself, graduating from a few short hops to full-blown flight. With the support of the Air League of the British Empire, a respected body that had been founded in 1909, Mignet produced a second book in which he set out detailed instructions on how to fly the Flea. The first edition of 6000 copies sold out in two weeks.

In Britain, the Flea craze gathered momentum. The grim, depressed years of the 1920s were fading into memory, and ordinary people once more had money to spend. Thanks to the efforts of organisations such as the Air League, Britain was becoming increasingly air-minded. Many people, no longer content to be thrilled by the exploits of others at air displays, now wanted to become amateur pilots themselves. The Flying Flea, it seemed, now placed that dream within the grasp of the ordinary man in the street – and woman too, for the activities of pilots such as Amy Johnson had given huge impetus to the place of women in the world of private flying.

Mignet continued to tour Britain, and people flocked to see him wherever his aircraft touched down. The Flying Flea now had some powerful advocates, including Air Commodore Chamier of the Air League, who built one for himself. The *Daily Express* published regular construction details, encouraging step-by-step, daily progress in hundreds of homes in the country. Fleas were being built from Land's End to John o'Groats. In many cases, amateur constructors took the basic design and incorporated their own modifications and improvements, so that very few Flying Fleas were exactly alike. By April 1936, eighty-one examples of the definitive version of the Flea, the HM-14, had appeared on the British civil aircraft register. The HM-14 Flying Flea was a very simple wooden machine. It had a spruce and ply box fuselage, to which was bolted the engine, and a straight-through axle was lashed to the longerons with elastic cord to provide springing for the barrow-wheel undercarriage. Engines of around 20 to 40 hp could be fitted, and a rudimentary chain reduction gear could be used with motorcycle engines to reduce the propeller shaft speed. The rear wing was bolted to the top of the fuselage immediately behind the cockpit cut-out. Although described as a tandem monoplane, the Flea was really a super-staggered tailless biplane, having two sharply-upswept wings of equal chord.

The front wing (Mignet called this 'the living wing' since it was the main control surface) could be built in three spans, depending on whether the machine was to be used for ground training hops, for circuits and bumps, or for serious tourist flying, in which case the large-span wing was used. The front wing also had a reflex trailing edge, which could be described as a full-span fixed elevon. Neither wing carried any form of movable control surface. The front wing was pivoted at the approximate centre of pressure, incidence being controlled directly by a cable attached to a lever on the control column layshaft. By moving the stick fore and aft, the wing could be tilted. When the aircraft was at rest on the ground, a 'bungee' cord attached to the leading edge of the wing prevented the front wing from flopping down to maximum incidence. In later Fleas, the incidence control cable was replaced by a control rod. The rudder was operated by moving the stick from side to side. The pilot's feet had nothing to do.

Several small firms set up their own production lines. Stephen Appleby formed Puttnam Aircraft Limited at Heston for this purpose. A furniture company produced Fleas; a firm started up in a mews in the heart of London and built eleven. Engines of almost every type were used. They included the 35 hp ABC Scorpion; 35 hp Anzani; 22 hp Aubier et Dunne; 847 cc. Austin Seven; 32 hp Bristol Cherub; 30 hp Carden-Ford; 30 hp Perman-Ford; 23 hp Douglas Sprite; 38 hp Menguin; 25 hp Poinsard; 36 hp Praga B; and the 25 hp Scott Flying Squirrel – a version of the famous motorcycle engine designed expressly for the Flea. The engine installation was intended to be completely uncowled, although some examples, notably those built by Puttnam Aircraft Limited and Perman Aircraft Limited, had fully cowled modified Ford car engines. A novel characteristic was that the aircraft could be towed along the road on its own undercarriage.

The apparent lack of concern for uniformity in Flea-building was causing concern among professional aircraft designers. They warned that under certain circumstances the Flea might prove dangerous, owing to there being insufficient pitching moment to raise the nose. Also, if the two wings were allowed to overlap each other when rigging to get the centre of gravity right, the front one would act as a slot to the rear one, increasing the lift on the rear wing as the incidence of the front wing increased. The effect would be a control reversal.

Many Fleas were involved in minor mishaps, and as early as January 1936 the Air League was attempting to solve the problem by urging builders to move the rear wing back by some 19 inches. For the most part, Flea constructors took no notice of such concerns.

On 6 April 1936, the first Flea meeting was held at Ashington by the Aero 8 Club. Among those present was the Austin Seven-powered Flea, G-AEEI; this particular Flea remained in use until 1939. Flea enthusiasts were invited to attend with their machines, irrespective of the state of their construction, and the majority of Fleas came by road. Those whose machines were complete spent the afternoon charging across the field, regardless of any traffic control or wind direction, trying to take off. As might be expected, there were numerous ground collisions, but nobody was hurt. One Flea had short-span wings and was available for hire to the public so they could charge across the field and experience the joys of the elastic cord undercarriage springing. It was not intended that it should fly, but it did, completely inadvertently and much to the delight of the small boy who happened to be in it at the time. The Flea was lifted by a gust of wind and landed forty feet up in a tree. The boy scrambled down, unhurt and jubilant.

Then the serious accidents began to happen. A fortnight after the Ashington meeting, on 20 April 1936, a Flea registered G-ADVL and owned by Mr H.H. Paterson took off from Renfrew, Scotland. Shortly afterwards, eyewitnesses saw the nose of the aircraft go down and the aircraft enter a dive that became gradually steeper until the Flea hit the ground, killing its owner-pilot. No serious investigation into the accident was carried out, and the cause remained undetermined. On 5 May, Flying Flea G-AEEW flown by Flight Lieutenant Cowell crashed at Penshurst in Kent under precisely the same circumstances, the pilot also being killed. On 21 May Flying Flea G-AEBS plunged into the ground at Digby, Lincolnshire, killing Squadron Leader C.R. Davidson. The close proximity of these accidents, two of which involved experienced airmen, and the similarity between them should have resulted in the grounding of all Flying Fleas while an investigation was carried out, but it did not. Instead, on 3 August 1936, the first ever Flying Flea race meeting was staged at Ramsgate. Four French and four British-built aircraft took part in the race and, although Stephen Appleby put up the fastest time at 59.9 mph, a French Flea won. Mignet himself was present with his latest Flea – the HM-8 cabin Pou du Ciel, which featured a small elevator set in the trailing edge of the rear wing. Appleby later bought this machine and flew it back to France as G-AENV, where it was exhibited at the Paris Air Show.

Another fatal accident involving a Flea occurred on 20 September 1936, when G-ADXY crashed at Dyce, Aberdeen, killing pilot James Goodall. The Air League, aware that a number of carbon-copy fatal crashes had also occurred in France, now decided to take action. The organisation sent Flying Flea G-AEFV, which was powered by the 25 hp Scott Flying Squirrel engine, to the Royal Aircraft Establishment at Farnborough for wind tunnel testing. These tests, and similar ones in France, came to the same conclusion. If the angle of attack (the angle at which the wing meets the airflow) of the forward wing exceeded –15°, insufficient pitching moment was generated to raise the nose. The result was a dive that became progressively steeper, and one from which the pilot was powerless to recover.

The French authorities immediately grounded all Flying Fleas, and the British Air Ministry followed suit in the summer of 1937. In Britain, 123 Fleas had been registered, of which 83 had received Permits to Fly. Many others operated unregistered; exactly how many will never be known.

Late in 1937 Henri Mignet, having been persuaded by a group of American businessmen, left for the United States, where he founded the American Mignet Aircraft Company in Chicago. In Britain and France, the hundreds of Fleas that had been lovingly built by enthusiastic amateurs ended their days as firewood, or were converted into chicken coops. At the beginning of the Second World War many Fleas that had been placed in storage were donated to the Air Defence Cadet Corps – which became the Air Training Corps in 1941 – for use as instructional airframes.

Henri Mignet tried to resurrect the Flying Flea concept after the war, and in June 1946 he published plans for a new variant, the HM-290. The design generated no enthusiasm, and attempts to promote it were not helped by wildly exaggerated stories that Mignet's pre-war Fleas had suffered structural failure in flight, causing dozens of fatalities.

Saddened by the death of his wife Annette in December 1944, Mignet became a virtual itinerant. In 1947 he left for Argentina, subsequently residing in Brazil, Japan and Morocco, before returning to France in 1957. Throughout his wanderings he never ceased his design work, always adhering to his principle that a light aircraft should be cheap, easy to build and have the ability to land 'like a parachute', as he put it, but he met with no success. He died of cancer on 31 August 1965, aged 71. Many of his Flying Fleas are preserved as museum pieces in Britain and France, monuments to a dream that, to this day, has still not been fulfilled.

CHAPTER FIVE

Me 209: the Deadly Record-breaker

In the spring of 1939, the Nazi propaganda machine broke the news that an aircraft designated Messerschmitt Me 109R had set a new world air speed record of 469.22 mph. The designation fostered the impression that the machine was a variant of Germany's new single-seat monoplane fighter, the Messerschmitt Bf 109. In fact, the "Me 109R" was the prototype of an entirely new aircraft, developed for the specific purpose of attacking the record. Its correct designation was Me 209V1, and it was one of the most dangerous aircraft ever built.

Developed at Messerschmitt's Augsburg factory, the Me 209 was a small, low-wing monoplane designed around a specially engineered Daimler-Benz DB 601ARJ twelve-cylinder inverted-vee liquid-cooled engine, which gave 1800 hp and could be boosted to 2300 hp for short periods. The airframe was kept as small as possible and equipment reduced to the absolute minimum. The pilot's cockpit was set well aft, the fin had a large ventral section, and the tailplane and elevators were very small in area. The wide-track undercarriage comprised two main members, retracting inwards into the wing and fuselage centre section, and a tailskid was fitted to the ventral fin.

In order to reduce drag to an absolute minimum, radiators were eliminated by introducing an engine evaporative cooling system. After passing around the engine, the water coolant was piped out to the wings, where it was cooled by partial evaporation through holes in the skin and then passed back into circulation. Because the system entailed a constant loss of water, at least 200 litres

(44 gallons) had to be carried on each flight, even though the engine could not be run for more than 30 minutes at a time.

The design bore the Messerschmitt project number P.1059. The prototype, which also carried the civil registration D-INJR and the *Werknummer* (Factory Number) 1185, flew for the first time on 1 August 1938, the pilot being Dr J.H. Wurster, who was then both chief engineer and chief test pilot at Augsburg. Some unpleasant characteristics became apparent from the beginning, notably the aircraft's tendency to nose down with no warning and for no apparent reason. The controls were heavy and unwieldy, the aircraft was generally unstable in flight, and the sink rate was high during the approach to land, resulting in a heavy touchdown and an inclination to swerve violently.

A second aircraft, the Me 209V2, D-IWAH, made its first flight on 4 April 1939. The role of chief test pilot had now been assumed by *Flugkapitän* Fritz Wendel, leaving Dr Wurster to concentrate on engineering matters. Wendel was less than enthusiastic about the little machine, and later described his impressions of it.

In 1937, our Bf 109Bs and Ds had caused a sensation at the Zurich International Flying meeting, winning many of the contests, and much of my early time as Chief Test Pilot was devoted to testing variants of this aircraft. Many an unkind word has been said about the flight characteristics of this little beauty, but it was a lady all through when compared to that winged horror with which I gained the world air speed record.

Adolf Hitler was determined that Germany should hold any and every aviation record, and he was particularly anxious that we should gain the absolute speed record. At that time the record had been established by Francesco Agello in a Macchi MC.72 seaplane at 440.7 mph. My predecessor, Dr Wurster, had raised the international landplane speed record to 379.39 mph on November 11, 1937, in a DB 600-powered Bf 109, but we were after the absolute record, and the result was the Me 209.

With its tiny wing and, for those days, horrifying wing loading, the 209 was a brute. Its flying characteristics still make me shudder. It had a dangerous tendency to nose down without any reason or warning, and it touched down on the runway like a ton of bricks. Even on the ground its characteristics were no more ladylike, as it would suddenly swerve off the runway without any provocation.

The first prototype, the Me 209V1, was initially fitted with a standard 1075 hp Daimler-Benz DB 601A in order to get some idea of the aircraft's flight characteristics before installing the specially souped-up engine for the record flight. This special engine delivered about 2300 hp for a short burst and then ... a new engine! Cooling presented Messerschmitt and the Daimler-Benz boys with a peach of a problem. Had orthodox radiators been fitted their drag would have seriously affected the plane's speed. Therefore, a surface evaporation cooling system was worked out. We knew that the working life of this souped-up engine would be but half an hour at the very most, and the engineers commandeered all the available space in the plane – which wasn't much – for water tanks. The water was run through the engine, out into the wing, condensed, and then back into the discharger. About one and a half gallons of water were consumed every minute of flying time, and the plane left a long trail of steam behind it!

On 4 April 1939, I took off for a training flight in preparation for the speed record attempt in the second prototype, the Me 209V2. After a few tiring minutes of heaving the unwieldy controls, I turned in for a landing approach. I was accustomed to lowering the undercarriage as I reached the Siebentischwald, a forest near the airfield at Haunstetten, but on that day, without warning (everything happened without warning in the Me 209) the lubricating system packed up, and immediately the pistons were grinding in the cylinders and the airscrew was standing as stiff as a poker. With a hell of a jolt, the plane virtually pulled up in mid-air, the result of the combined drag of the lowered undercarriage and the unfeathered airscrew. The vicious little brute started dropping like a stone, and below me was that damned forest. I strained on the stick with all I had and, to my surprise, the plane responded. I screamed over the last row of trees bordering the Haunstetterstrasse, and was even more surprised to find myself staggering away, relatively unhurt, from the heap of twisted metal that seconds before had been an Me 209.

A few days before this crash, on 30 March, Heinkel's test pilot, Hans Dieterle, captured the absolute speed record at 463.92 mph in our major competitor, the He 100V-8. So we had been forced to set our sights higher, and we knew that if we did raise the record still further it would be marginal. On 26 April 1939, only twenty-two days after my crash, I climbed into the cockpit of the blue-painted Me 209V1, now fitted with the souped-up engine, for an attempt to beat Dieterle. The engine sparked into life with its characteristic roar. A very brief warm-up, a last instrument check, and I was off, searing up and down the course and screeching round the clearly marked turning points. I touched down again and saw a crowd of workers and technicians racing towards the plane. I climbed out of the cockpit, and Willi Messerschmitt slapped me on the back and told me that we had 'got it'. The Me 209, as I was to discover later, had averaged 469.22 mph.

The record-breaking Me 209 was one of the most vicious aircraft ever designed.

Originally, it had been intended that the record attempt would be made by the third prototype Me 209, the V3 (D-IVFP, *Werknummer* 1187), but as this was not ready in time the V1 was used instead. The record was to stand for thirty years, until 16 August 1969, when it was beaten by American pilot Darryl G. Greenamyer, who achieved an average speed of 482.533 mph in his Grumman F8F-2 Bearcat, Conquest I.

The Me 209V3 eventually flew at the end of May 1939 and was used for experimental flying. With the coming of war in September 1939 all thoughts of further record-breaking attempts were abandoned, and the fourth prototype Me 209, the V4 (D-IRND, *Werknummer* 1188) was completed as a fighter. The Me 209V4 first flew on 12 May 1939 and had a redesigned wing with automatic leading edge slats. Provision was made for the installation of two nose-mounted 7.9 mm MG 17 machine-guns and one 30 mm MK 108 cannon (at a later date, an attempt was made to install two additional MK 108 cannon in the wings). After eight test flights the surface evaporation cooling system was abandoned in favour of a more orthodox arrangement of underwing radiators; the wing span was progressively increased and the slats were replaced by drooping leading edges. Further flight testing, however, revealed that the Me 209V4 could not attain its original estimated performance expectations and offered no great advantage over the standard Messerschmitt Bf 109.

The story of the Me 209, however, had by no means ended. Early in 1941, the Augsburg design team began to study a potential replacement for the Bf 109. Allocated the designation Me 309, the new fighter was of advanced concept, featuring a pressurised cockpit, tricycle undercarriage and retractable radiator. The new type incorporated a number of lessons learned during the Me 209 development programme, and various features were tested on modified Bf 109s. Because of all the innovations development was slow, and it was not until the end of 1941 that design work was completed.

The first prototype, the Me 309V1, began taxiing trials on 27 June 1942 and snags immediately manifested themselves. First of all, the coolant feed lines fractured, and it was found that they had been mounted too rigidly to withstand engine vibrations. No sooner had this fault been rectified than a serious nosewheel shimmy developed during ground runs. This, together with a directional snaking problem, delayed the prototype's maiden flight until 18 July 1942. Meanwhile, official interest in the project had waned, and production of the Me 309 was restricted to an experimental series of nine aircraft, not all of which were built. After the directional snaking and other problems had been sorted out the Me 309V1 was put through its paces at the *Luftwaffe* Experimental Establishment, Rechlin, where it was flown with a 1450 hp DB 605B engine in place of its original 1750 hp DB 603A. Rechlin test pilots were critical of its potential, one of them reporting that:

> *The Me 309 will be acceptable after certain improvements have been effected, but it should be stressed that this fighter will provide the average service pilot with handling difficulties. Control forces are very high by comparison with those of current fighters, and the nosewheel undercarriage is likely to present problems when the fighter uses operational airfields. With full armament, the Me 309 will be only some 30 mph faster than the Bf 109G, and there would seem to be no advantage to introducing this fighter when superior types (e.g. the Fw 190D) are already leaving the assembly lines.*

The second prototype, the Me 309V2, which was intended for high-speed trials, made its first flight on 29 November 1942. It was also its last, because the nosewheel leg collapsed during landing and the aircraft was damaged beyond repair. The test programme planned for the V2 could therefore not be implemented until the completion of the Me 309V3 in March 1943, by which time the radical Me 262 jet fighter was undergoing flight trials. The Me

Fitted with a tricycle undercarriage, which caused constant problems, the Me 309 was not a success.

309V3 was assigned to the Me 262 programme, testing cockpit pressurisation systems and ejector seats.

The last Me 309 prototype, the V4, flew in July 1943 and was used exclusively as an armament trials aircraft. It was fitted with four MG131, two MG151/20 and two MK108 guns in the wings and fuselage. It was destroyed in an air raid.

The Me 209V-5, also designated Me 209A, was an unsuccessful replacement for the Bf 109 and bore no resemblance to the record-breaking Me 209.

Incredibly, despite Messerschmitt's failure to develop a viable fighter from the Me 209, in the summer of 1943 the German Air Ministry (RLM) resurrected the Me 209 designation and ordered Messerschmitt to proceed with the design of a new fighter, to be designated Me 209V5. It was proposed to equip the aircraft with the DB 603G engine, featuring an annular radiator, which would produce an improved cooling effect. New and enlarged vertical tail surfaces would, it was believed, rectify the tendency to swing during take-off, which had been an adverse feature of Messerschmitt's earlier single-engined fighter designs, while a new wide-track undercarriage was to be introduced. The type also featured a wing of increased span and area; wing loading was some 25 per cent higher than that of the Bf 109G.

The first prototype of the new fighter, which bore no resemblance to the original Me 209, flew for the first time on 3 November 1943, with Fritz Wendel at the controls. A second prototype, the Me 209V6, made its first flight on 22 December 1943, and a third aircraft began flights tests in May 1944. This was intended to be the first pre-production aircraft and was designated Me 209A2, but further development was abandoned in favour of the Focke-Wulf Fw 190D, which was about to enter full production. Nevertheless, Messerschmitt went ahead with a fourth prototype, the Me 209HV1, which had a high aspect ratio wing and was intended as a high-altitude interceptor. This aircraft flew in June 1944 and was used as a flying test bed, the Focke-Wulf Ta 152 having been selected to fulfil the high-altitude interceptor role.

As for the original record-breaking Me 209, its airframe – minus wings and engine – was seized by the Polish Army in 1945. It now reposes in the Polish National Aircraft Museum, Krakow.

CHAPTER SIX

Trouble with Engines: the Avro Manchester and Hawker Typhoon

I n November 1936, the British Air Ministry issued Specification P13/36, which called for a bomber capable of carry a load greater than 8000 lb and powered by a pair of the new Rolls Royce X-type engines, then under development. A further requirement was that the aircraft must have a dive-bombing capability at angles of up to 30 degrees – a requirement that, oddly enough, was also built into the specifications of new German heavy bombers such as the Heinkel He 177 in the late 1930s. The overall result was that the aircraft had to be structurally strengthened, which in the case of the He 177 led to unacceptable weight penalties. The Air Ministry specification also stipulated that the bomb bay was to be large enough to permit the carriage of two 18-inch torpedoes.

The Manchester heavy bomber proposed by Avro was an outstanding design from the airframe point of view, but the engines selected to power it were a cause for concern from the very beginning. The best engine then available was the Rolls-Royce Merlin, but two of these would not provide sufficient power for an aircraft of the size and weight of the Manchester. In any case, the whole of Merlin production was allocated to RAF Fighter Command's new monoplane fighters, the Hawker Hurricane and

Supermarine Spitfire. Consequently, Avro had little choice but to take a gamble and opt for the Rolls-Royce X-Type, soon to be named the Vulture, which was still in the development stage. The 24-cylinder Vulture was, in fact, a marriage of two Rolls-Royce Peregrine engines, one inverted on top of the other, driving a single crankshaft and served by a complex lubricating system. As an insurance against the failure of the Vulture, Avro produced revised designs for the Manchester to accommodate other engines such as the Napier 24-valve radial then in design, as well as a four-engined version with Merlins.

The first flight of the Manchester was delayed by successive design changes ordered by Rolls-Royce as they revised the Vulture during 1938, but the aircraft finally took to the air on 25 July 1939. Although the engines performed well, the aircraft suffered from poor control and a long take-off, even though no armament was fitted. Changes were made to the second aircraft to rectify the control problems, namely increasing the wingspan and adding a small fin on the rear fuselage. These changes had little effect on control but the take-off run was shortened. With orders for the Manchester standing at 1200 and Rolls-Royce increasingly under pressure to concentrate on Merlin production, work on the four-engined airframe continued and showed that control could be improved by increasing the size of the twin rudders.

In August 1940, the first production aircraft was flown to Boscombe Down for tests. The engines were derated in an effort to improve reliability and the first Manchesters were cleared for service with No. 207 Squadron at Waddington. The squadron's work-up to operational readiness was severely hampered by the unreliability of the Vulture engines, and a great deal of concern was voiced when the aircraft was used in the dive-bombing role originally called for by the Air Ministry. No. 207 Squadron's first operational sortie with the Manchester was flown on the night of 24/25 February 1941, when six aircraft were despatched with fifty-one other bombers to attack enemy warships at Brest. There were no losses due to enemy action, but one Manchester crashed in England after its engines caught fire. No losses were sustained two nights later, when No. 207 Squadron's Manchesters formed part of a 126-strong bomber force that attacked Cologne.

Because of recurring engine problems, operations by the Manchesters were very sporadic. It was not until the night of 12/13 March 1941 that No. 207 Squadron was active again, sending four aircraft to Hamburg. On the following night the squadron lost its first Manchester to enemy action, when an aircraft captained by Flying Officer Hugh Matthews was shot down by an intruder as it took off from Waddington for another attack on Hamburg. Only one crew member survived.

No. 207 Squadron was now joined by a second Manchester squadron, No. 97, which began re-equipping in March 1941. Both squadrons joined in Bomber Command's offensive, which at this time was directed principally against German warships and their ports, but continued problems with the Vulture engines meant that the Manchesters were frequently grounded. It was a relatively common occurrence for a Manchester crew to complete a sortie to Germany or the French Atlantic ports without trouble, only to have their aircraft's engines overheat uncontrollably as they returned to base, often with disastrous results.

In April 1941, when all forty Manchesters then in service were grounded to have engine bearings replaced, it was discovered that repeated overheating of the Vultures was causing the oil to lose its viscosity in one-fifth of the expected time. This accounted for the frequent engine seizures that were being experienced. Morale, understandably, was not at its best in the Manchester squadrons.

More Manchester squadrons continued to form, however. No. 61 Squadron received its first aircraft in July 1941; these were Mk 1As, featuring larger fins, which cured the poor handling of earlier aircraft. Four other squadrons, Nos 83, 106, 50 and 49 also received Manchesters by the end of the year. By that time, the trouble-plagued bombers were regular participants in operations over Germany with bomb loads of up to 8000 lb, but more often than not they were restricted to attacking German naval vessels in the Channel ports with armour-piercing bombs.

The last operational Manchester sortie, a raid by a single aircraft on Bremen, was flown on the night of 25/26 June 1942. Of the 1200 Manchesters that had originally been ordered from Avro, only 200 had been delivered before the type was withdrawn.

While production of the Manchester was in progress, one airframe, BT308, was designated a 'four-engined Manchester' and fitted with four Rolls-Royce Merlin XX engines. It first flew on 9 January 1941 with triple fins and without ventral or dorsal turrets, and was the prototype of an aircraft that would become a legend: the Avro Lancaster.

The feelings of a typical aircrew member about the Avro Manchester were expressed by Flight Lieutenant Bob Jones, a former wireless operator air gunner who had flown in Handley Page Hampdens and then Manchesters.

In No. 207 Squadron, the disastrous Manchester was soon replaced by its illustrious four-engined successor, the Lancaster.

The only time I started to get really frightened was when we converted on to Manchesters. During my very first trip in a Manchester the port engine burst into flames and we scraped in by the skin of our teeth. On another occasion we took a Manchester from Waddington to Boscombe Down to have some equipment fitted, and were marooned there for a week because the engines wouldn't start. Soon after that I went sick and was in hospital for three months. I'm convinced to this day that it saved my life; I lost a hell of a lot of good mates in Manchesters. They were bastards.

Another design that had unfortunate experiences with the Vulture engine was the Hawker Tornado. In 1936 the Hawker design team at Kingston, under the leadership of Sydney Camm, prepared two versions of a common fighter design, similar in every respect but for the engine mountings and cowlings. One aircraft was designed to take the Rolls-Royce Vulture, and was designated Type R; the other, the Type N, was to be powered by another new high-performance engine, the Napier Sabre.

The Hawker proposal was submitted to the Air Ministry in January 1937, but no action was taken by that department until January 1938, when Specification F18/37 was issued. This covered the design of a new interceptor fighter. Hawker immediately submitted their Type R/Type N proposal afresh. The Hawker tenders were accepted on 22 April 1938 and two prototypes of each aircraft were ordered on 30 August that year.

The Vulture-powered Type R, now known as the Tornado, was the first to fly, on 6 October 1939. The prototype, P5219, had a ventral radiator, a large cockpit rear fairing and a Hurricane-type fin. Originally powered by a Vulture II engine, it was fitted with a Vulture V in March 1941. This developed 2060 hp and gave the aircraft a maximum speed of 423 mph at 23,000 feet. The proposed fixed armament was twelve 0.303 in Browning machine-guns or four 20 mm Hispano cannon.

Early tests with P5219 revealed that the airflow around the outside of the ventral radiator and that over the fuselage and wings interfered with one another, resulting in very high local velocities, particularly at the thick wing roots. Problems with compressibility – the first time this phenomenon had been experienced – manifested themselves in a sharp increase in drag, accompanied by violent shuddering and vibration at speeds approaching 400 mph IAS (indicated airspeed). Photographs showed that wool tufts attached to the rear half of the radiator were actually being blown forwards. To cure the problem the radiator was moved forward to a position immediately below the Vulture engine, necessitating a complete redesign of the nose. In its new guise, P5219 was reserialled P5224.

One thousand Tornadoes had been ordered within eight days of the prototype's first flight, and a production line for 1000 aircraft was set up by A.V. Roe (Avro), the principal subcontractor. Problems with the Vulture engine, however, continued to mount, and the operational debut of the Avro Manchester revealed even more hitherto unsuspected troubles, such as coolant circulation problems and big-end failures owing to defects in the oil circulation system. It was therefore decided to terminate production of the Vulture and cancel the Tornado production order, although the first and only Avro-built aircraft, HG641, eventually flew on 23 October 1941 fitted with a Bristol Centaurus radial engine. Its flight test programme provided much useful information in the development of the Centaurus-engined Hawker Tempest F.Mk.II.

Meanwhile, Hawker's second proposal to specification F18/37, the 2200 hp Sabre-engined Type N prototype, now named Typhoon, had made a successful maiden flight on 24 February 1940. Soon afterwards, the Sabre engine went into full production stride; in 1940 Lord Beaverbrook was made Minister of Aircraft Production, and he immediately saw the promise of the Sabre and commandeered facilities for its manufacture. From having practically nothing, Napier suddenly found themselves with an almost embarrassing supply of premises. There were, however, no sudden floods of Sabres, because as yet there were no airframes to accommodate them.

The prototype Typhoon, P5212, was followed by the second aircraft, P5216; by this time, like the unsuccessful Tornado, it had been ordered into quantity production. The Gloster Aircraft Company Ltd at Hucclecote, Gloucester, had been selected as the principal subcontractor. It was originally hoped that the Typhoon, which was of all-metal stressed-skin construction, would be in RAF squadron

The complex nature of the massive Napier Sabre engine is well illustrated in this photograph, showing the power plant installed in a Hawker Tempest V.

service by July 1940, but the first production Typhoon Mk IA did not fly until May 1941. Delays in production were blamed on the unreliability of the Sabre engine. However, there were other problems, including a near-catastrophic structural failure of the rear fuselage of P5212, which test pilot Philip Lucas landed safely with great skill and earned himself a well-deserved George Medal.

The Typhoon's entry into service was inauspicious. The first squadron to equip with the aircraft – No. 56, at Duxford, in September 1941 – was bedevilled by continual engine problems and structural failures, losing several pilots. Moreover, although the aircraft was fast and handled well at medium and low altitudes, its performance at high altitude was inferior to that of both the Focke-Wulf Fw 190 and the Messerschmitt Bf 109F, and its rate of climb was poor. Teething troubles kept the squadron non-operational with the type until the end of May 1942, and at one time there was talk of cancelling the Typhoon programme altogether.

There are experts who have suggested that many of the problems encountered with the Typhoon were caused by lack of expertise in handling the new complex Sabre, rather than technical defects in the engine itself. One such was L.J.K. Setright, who in his book *The Power to Fly* (Allen & Unwin, 1971) wrote:

> By the time it came into service all too many of the really good Fighter Command pilots had gone, and those who had taken their places were generally of poorer quality and were usually given the most hasty and superficial training before being sent out to do battle... When they

encountered difficulties with the Sabre they condemned what they did not understand. In fact the engine only presented two serious problems in all its service career, a record considerably less expensive than that of any other engine that springs to mind. One was a certain difficulty in starting when it was very cold. The sleeves were a very tight fit until the cylinder blocks had expanded a little as they grew warm, and many of the internal bearings were fairly tight too, so that at about freezing point or a little below it became virtually impossible to turn the engine over with its Coffman cartridge starter to get it running. The proper technique was to resort to oil dilution, a practice regularly employed by the Germans, and a simple tap in the cockpit discharged the correct amount of petrol into the lubricant in order to achieve this. Even then there were difficulties, for most of the pilots and many of the mechanics were completely unversed in the operation of the Kigass priming system and would usually mishandle it. So with one thing and another, coupled with the tendency to oil leakage inevitable because of the purblind refusal of the Air Ministry to accept paper gaskets in the joints of British-made aero-engines, although they accepted American-built Merlins with such gaskets (and although they did not know it, Napier often slipped them in when no one was looking!) a misfire or failure to get running properly when starting up from cold could have fiery consequences. Many trainee pilots were absolutely terrified of their Typhoons, largely because of this.

Problems with the Typhoon's tail persisted, and twenty-eight aircraft were lost through structural failure of the rear fuselage before the cause was isolated. One of the problems facing the accident investigators was that no failure had occurred during a high-speed dive or other manoeuvre, which put the greatest strain on the airframe. Eventually it was found that the failures had been caused by 'flutter' induced in the elevators, building up to such an extent that it tore off the rear fuselage. The root cause was metal fatigue in a bracket and the positioning of the mass balance within the elevator. Once the fault had been located, the cure was relatively simple.

Wing Commander Roland Beamont, whose role in operationally testing the Typhoon was crucial to the ultimate success of the aircraft, flew the Hawker Tornado prototypes while engaged in Hurricane production testing at Hawkers in 1942. His first flight in a Typhoon was made on 8 March 1942 in a Mk IA with twelve machine-guns. He had this to say about the experience in *Fighter Test Pilot* (Patrick Stephens Ltd, 1986).

... Once it was established that the noise, vibration and general commotion caused by the big Sabre engine and enhanced by the draughty cockpit with rattling 'wind-up' side windows was not actually

Hawker Typhoon fighter-bombers, wearing D-Day invasion stripes, waiting to depart on operations over Normandy.

breaking or stopping anything, it was soon apparent that the aeroplane was pleasantly stable and responsive to controls in all axes, very manoeuvrable (and exceptionally so for that period at speeds above 400 mph) and it had a tremendous turn of speed. A 75 per cent power low-level cruise at over 300 mph was fast for those days as was a massive power 'level' of 385 mph; and at the advertised dive limit of 500mph there was adequate control remaining, though with heavy control forces and an impressive noise level.

High speed, however, could produce its own dangers, as one test pilot, E.W. 'Jock' Bonar discovered when he put a Typhoon through a series of high-speed dives to investigate oil scavenging problems. Rolling into a dive at 35,000 feet, the Typhoon accelerated vertically, very fast. Suddenly, there was a complete loss of control: the elevators, rudder and ailerons were all completely ineffective. Bonar managed to pull out using the elevator trimmers and regained full control as the aircraft descended into denser air, and was shocked to see that the skin on the wings was shuddering and flapping. Bonar landed safely, but the Typhoon was a complete write-off, the victim of an as yet unknown effect called compressibility.

In the summer of 1942, three squadrons of Typhoons – Nos 56, 266 and 609, the three forming the Duxford Wing – operated successfully against Focke-Wulf Fw 190s and Messerschmitt Bf 109s carrying out fast hit-and-run attacks on ports and other targets on the south coast of England. On 20 January 1943 the Typhoon at last showed what it could do as an interceptor. On that day twenty-eight enemy fighter-bombers, escorted by single-engined fighters, made a daylight attack on London, while diversionary attacks were made on the Isle of Wight and the Kent coast. The balloon barrage had been grounded before the raid, and there was so little warning of the incoming enemy that the defences were taken almost completely by surprise.

However, the Typhoons of No. 609 Squadron were scrambled in

The wreckage of a Focke-Wulf Fw 190 intruder, shot down by Typhoons over the south coast.

time to intercept the raiders on the way out. In the ensuing fight Flying Officer Johnny Baldwin – later to become the top-scoring Typhoon pilot – destroyed three Bf 109Gs, while three Fw 190s were shot down by three other No. 609 Squadron pilots.

Several more successes were achieved against the enemy fighter-bombers by No. 609 Squadron in the weeks that followed. During this period the squadron also continued to expand its offensive operations against targets on the Continent. There was no longer any doubt about the Typhoon's effectiveness at low level, and No. 609 Squadron's performance under the command of Roland Beamont effectively killed a last-ditch attempt by the Engineering Branch of Fighter Command, early in 1943, to have the fighter-bomber axed in favour of the American Republic P-47 Thunderbolt. By the end of the year, with the aircraft's technical problems cured and the growing number of Typhoon squadrons – now carrying a pair of 500 lb bombs on their machines in addition to the built-in cannon armament – striking hard at the enemy's airfields, communications and shipping, the Typhoon was heading for its place in history as the most potent Allied fighter-bomber of all.

A rocket-armed Typhoon Mk IB of No. 198 Squadron, which equipped with the type in December 1942.

C H A P T E R   S E V E N

Terrible Twins

The Messerschmitt Me 210

Without doubt, the worst twin-engined combat aircraft to emerge from Germany's wartime industry was the Messerschmitt Me 210, which started life as a 1937 project for a multi-purpose aircraft to replace the Bf 110. Even at this early stage of its development, the latter aircraft, which had flown in 1936, was showing ominous signs that it would not reach its projected performance expectations and would probably not be wholly adequate for the long-range heavy fighter role for which it had been designed. A *Reichsluftministerium* (RLM) specification was issued to cover the new design and three companies – Ago, Arado and Messerschmitt – submitted proposals. However, the Ago design, the Ao 225, was technically too complex and the company was experiencing financial problems, which led to its early abandonment. The other two designs, the Arado Ar 240 and the Me 210, were approved while still on the drawing board. The Ar 240 first flew in May 1940; the first four prototypes were fighters, the next four reconnaissance aircraft, and the final one a night fighter. The initial production model, the Ar 240A-0, was a high-altitude reconnaissance aircraft, while the Ar 240B-0 was built in both fighter-bomber and reconnaissance versions. The Ar 240C was a projected multi-role model, while the Ar 240E and F were respectively bomber and fighter developments. During operational trials, Ar 240A-0s made reconnaissance sorties over England and Russia. However, the type suffered from continual handling problems, and after limited use in the reconnaissance role it disappeared from operational service, plans for large-scale production having been cancelled in 1942.

The Me 210V-1 prototype flew for the first time on 2 September 1939, powered by two 1100 hp Daimler-Benz DB 601A engines. This aircraft, and the two subsequent prototypes, were originally fitted with twin fins and rudders. However, early test flights revealed marked longitudinal instability and these features were replaced by a large single fin. The V2 and V3 prototypes also had a redesigned cockpit. They were fitted with mock-ups of the Rheinmetall-Borsig FDL 131 remotely controlled defensive gun barbettes on either side of the fuselage aft of the wing trailing edge, the cockpit canopy being bulged so that the gunner could see downwards and to the rear. It had a large bomb bay in the nose, which could accommodate up to 2200 lb of bombs or alternatively six 20 mm cannon. For the dive-bombing role, the aircraft was fitted with a Stuvi 5B bomb sight.

Although the single fin and rudder arrangement improved the Me 210's flight characteristics somewhat, it still continued to display some seriously bad habits, including a tendency to stall at the slightest provocation. At high angles of attack, or in a turn, a stall would develop into a vicious spin.

One thousand examples of the Me 210 had been ordered straight off the drawing board. The wisdom of this decision was soon questioned. In the opinion of Messerschmitt test pilot Fritz Wendel, fresh from his unhappy experiences with the record-breaking Me 209, the Me 210:

... was nearly as bad as Heinkel's He 177, surely the worst plane we produced in Germany throughout the war years. I was never happy about the Me 210. I have only been forced to bale out of an aircraft twice, and the first time was from this twin-engined fighter-bomber.

It was on 5 September 1940, that I took off from Augsburg-Haunstetten in the Me 210V-2. We had more than a suspicion that the tail assembly was weak, and that there was a strong possibility that it would part company with the rest of the airfame in a dive. I was flying solo, the mechanic who usually occupied the radio operator's seat on test flights being left on the ground as this flight was likely to be more than usually dangerous.

During the climb I recall the thought flashing through my mind: 'If something goes wrong, remember to avoid baling out over the forest.' At 9000 feet I checked my instruments and started the planned series of dives, my unpleasant thoughts temporarily forgotten. Stick forward ... down went the nose and the needle began to creep round the airspeed indicator. Stick back, and the nose lifted. Stick forward ... back ... forward, and so on. One more shallow dive and back to the airfield. A thousand feet showed on the altimeter and I began to level off. Then it happened, and right over that blasted Siebentischwald again! The plane shuddered, the tail fluttered, and bang, the starboard elevator broke off! Immediately the plane went into a half-loop downwards. Before I could gather my wits I was flying on my back in the direction from which I had just come. I knew exactly what would happen now, as I had seen the same thing happen to the first prototype some weeks before. The plane would fly inverted for several seconds and then dive straight into the ground.

Hanging on my seat straps, head downwards, I automatically grabbed the release pin, but I hadn't jettisoned the canopy. In that split second I fumbled for the roof's emergency release lever, pulled it, and the canopy flew off with a bang. I pulled the release pin ... the chute opened with a glorious crack. I looked down, and there were those damned trees almost touching my feet. But I was in luck, for the wind blew me towards the only clearing that I could see, and I escaped with nothing worse than a sprained ankle. I had lost a prototype, but at least I had proved its unstatisfactory characteristics and had lived to tell the tale. But there are few things in the world harder than proving to an aircraft designer that his latest pet creation in simply not good enough.

Despite the dangerous shortcomings that became apparent during the testing of the Me 210 prototypes, the RLM ordered a batch of pre-production Me 210A-0 aircraft. They were intended for *Erprobungsgruppe* 210 (EGr 210), the special *Luftwaffe* unit that had been formed at Köln-Ostheim under the command of *Hauptmann* Walter Rubensdörffer on 7 July 1940 for the specific purpose of pioneering the Me 210's entry into full operational service. One of the unit's *Staffeln*, I/EGr 210, was equipped with the Messerschmitt Bf 110C, and was activated by simply renumbering I/*Zerstörergeschwader* 1 (I/ZG 1); similarly, III/*Stukageschwader 77*, which was armed with the Messerschmitt Bf 110D, became II/EGr 210. The group's third *Staffel*, equipped with Messerschmitt Bf 109Es, was previously IV/*Trägergruppe* 186, which had been designated as the fighter element of the air group intended for the aircraft carrier *Graf Zeppelin*, on which work had been halted. EGr 210 had been operationally active during the Battle of Britain, carrying out precision attacks on targets such as radar stations and RAF airfields, and the losses sustained by its Bf 110 fighter-bombers had served to underline the fact that the type was outmoded.

EGr 210 received its first Me 210A-0s at the end of 1940, but although the unit was still based in the English Channel area, the new aircraft were not used operationally against the British Isles.

In April 1941 the unit was redesignated *Schnellkampfgeschwader* 210 (SKG 210), and a month later it moved to Poland under Major Walter Storp for the start of the campaign in Russia. In April 1942 it was absorbed into Zerstörergeschwader 1, disbanding in July 1944.

The first unit to use the Me 210 operationally, in fact, was *Zerstörergeschwader* 1, whose II *Gruppe* equipped with the type late in 1941 and served on the Eastern Front. The Me 210 was also operated by 10/ZG 26 in Tunisia and III/ZG 1 on the Italian front. There were two major production sub-types, the Me 210A-1 heavily armed 'destroyer' and the Me 210A-2 fighter-bomber; four examples of a photo-reconnaissance variant, the Me 210B-1, were also built, and these served with 2(F)/122. The Me 210 was also built under licence in Hungary, and was used by the 102nd Fast Attack Bomber group of the Royal Hungarian Air Force. Most of the Me 210s built in Hungary were the Me 210C variant, which was basically an A or B model with 1475 hp DB 605B engines. About two-thirds of the Hungarian production went to the *Luftwaffe*.

In April 1942, production of the Me 210 in Germany was halted after only ninety aircraft had been delivered to operational units, a decision dictated by the aircraft's phenomenal accident rate. Production was resumed in July, after the aircraft had been fitted with leading-edge slots, a modification that substantially improved its flight characteristics.

In the summer of 1942 an experimental unit designated *Versuchstaffel* (Trials Squadron) 210 formed at Soesterberg, Holland, for operations against the British Isles. This unit became operational as 16 *Staffel*/KG 6 in August. On 13 August 1942, the first Me 210 to be shot down over England was destroyed by Flight Lieutenant A.C. Johnston, flying a Hawker Typhoon of No. 266 Squadron; the combat took place east of Cromer. Two more Me 210s were shot down by Typhoons of the same squadron on 6 September, off the Yorkshire coastal resorts of Robin Hood's Bay and Redcar. It was the end of the Me 210's brief and unspectacular combat career against Britain.

Late in 1942, after 352 examples had been built, production of the Me 210 switched to an improved version, the Me 410 Hornisse (Hornet). This aircraft was essentially an Me 210 incorporating all the latter's hard-earned modifications and equipped with two Daimler-Benz DB 603A engines. As well as being used in the fast bomber role, the Me 410 was used as a night fighter and a bomber destroyer, being armed with a 50 mm cannon in the latter case. We can see a measure of what they might have achieved, had these aircraft been committed in greater numbers, in one attack on American air bases in East Anglia on 2 April 1944. Me 410s destroyed thirteen B-24 Liberators and, in the panic, two more were shot down by their own airfield defences. The Germans lost a single Me 410.

By the beginning of 1944, however, further improvements in the British air defences had made it hard for the *Luftwaffe* to penetrate UK air space at medium and low level. Increased numbers of anti-aircraft guns of all calibres, rocket batteries capable of firing salvoes of 128 missiles, and radar-directed searchlights able to illuminate targets up to 35,000 feet all contributed to frustrating the attackers. The fast enemy bombers now began to penetrate at altitudes up to 30,000 feet before diving on their objectives and making a high-speed exit. These new tactics caused problems for the British night fighters, since following an enemy aircraft in a dive meant that radar contact was often lost because of ground returns. The answer was to extend the night-fighter patrol lines well out to sea; many intruders were trapped and destroyed in this way. Between 13 July 1943 and 5 June 1944, forty-three Me 410s were shot down by Mosquito night fighters during night operations against England; many more were to be destroyed during subsequent operations over the Continent.

Martin B-26 Marauder

Another twin-engined bomber that experienced severe handling problems, and a phenomenal accident rate in its early days, was the Martin B-26 Marauder. However, in this case the eventual outcome was somewhat happier. One of the most controversial Allied medium bombers of the Second World War, at least in the early stages of its career, the Glenn L. Martin 179 was entered in a US Army light and medium bomber competition in 1939. Its designer, Peyton M. Magruder, placed the emphasis on high speed, producing an aircraft with a torpedo-like fuselage, two massive radial engines, tricycle undercarriage and stubby wings. The advanced nature of the aircraft's design proved so impressive that an immediate order was placed for 201 examples off the drawing board, without a prototype. The first B-26 flew on 25 November 1940, powered by two Pratt & Whitney R-2800-5 engines; by this time, orders for 1131 B-26A and B-26B bombers had been received, and training establishments had been set up at MacDill Field, Tampa, Florida and Barksdale Field, Louisiana.

The first unit to rearm with a mixture of B-26s and B-26As was the 22nd Bombardment Group (BG) at Langley Field in February 1941. Early in 1942 it moved to Australia, where it became part of the US Fifth Air Force, attacking enemy shipping, airfields and installations in New Guinea and New Britain. It carried out its first attack, a raid on Rabaul, on 5 April 1942. During the Battle of Midway in June, four B-26As of the 22nd and 38 th BG attacked units of the Japanese fleet with torpedoes.

Meanwhile, at the B-26 training bases in the United States, all was far from well. Many of the pilots reporting for training on the B-26 had no previous twin-engined experience, and soon the accident rate had reached such a level that the Marauder's future was placed seriously in jeopardy. Most of the accidents occurred during the take-off or landing phase; the increases in weight that had been gradually introduced on the B-26 production line had made the wing loading of the Marauder progressively higher. This resulted in higher stalling and landing speeds, which novice twin-engine pilots found difficult to master. Before long, the B-26 had earned itself an unenviable reputation as a 'widowmaker' and a 'flying coffin'. Early in 1942, the accident level at MacDill had become so serious that the expression 'one a day into Tampa Bay' became commonplace.

Such was the concern about the Marauder's accident rate in senior USAAF circles that there was discussion about ceasing production of the type and withdrawing it from service. The US Senate's Special Committee to Investigate the National Defense Program (better known as the Truman Committee, after its chairman, Senator Harry S. Truman), which had been charged with ferreting out corruption, waste and mismanagement in the military procurement effort, also began looking into the Marauder's safety record. By July 1942, the committee had heard so many Marauder horror stories that they recommended production be stopped. However, combat crews in the South Pacific, who were more experienced, were not reporting any particular problems with the aircraft, and they campaigned for the Marauder. They exerted pressure, and the USAAF decided to continue production of the Marauder.

The situation at the training establishments, however, continued to worsen, with accidents becoming even more frequent. By September 1942, the B-26 had acquired such a bad reputation that even civilian crews under contract to ferry the type to its various destinations were refusing to fly the type, often losing their jobs as a consequence. A full investigation into the Marauder's disastrous loss rate was initiated by the USAAF's Air Safety Board, and in October the Truman Committee recommended that production should cease. By no means convinced that this decision was the right one, General H.H. Arnold, Commanding General of the USAAF, stepped in at this juncture. He turned the investigation over to Brigadier General James H. Doolittle, who in April 1942 had led sixteen B-25 Mitchell bombers, flown off the carrier USS *Hornet*, in a daring raid on Japan.

Doolittle was exactly the right man for the task. One of the leading pioneers of American aviation, he had learned to fly with the US Army in 1918. In the years after the First World War his flying career had been marked by a number of notable 'firsts'. He had become the first man to span the American continent with a flight from Florida to California; the first American to pilot an aircraft solely by instruments from take-off to landing; the first American to fly an outside loop; and in 1925 he had won the coveted Schneider Trophy for the United States. He had also been a test pilot for the Army Air Corps, had demonstrated American fighter designs overseas, and – of vital importance to his new assignment – he had obtained the degree of a Doctor of Science in aeronautical engineering at the Massachusetts Institute of Technology. During 1941, General Arnold, an old friend, used him as a kind of trouble-shooter to deal with the hundreds of problems that arose as the US aircraft industry strove to gear up its resources to meet the growing demand for modern aircraft by the armed forces. Doolittle now had a personal interest in the Marauder, as he had recently been given command of the B-26-equipped 4th Medium Bombardment Wing, which was scheduled to take part in the invasion of North Africa.

Doolittle's conclusion, supported by the Air Safety Board, was that there was nothing intrinsically wrong with the B-26, and there was no reason why it should be discontinued. They traced the problem to the inexperience of both aircrews and ground crews, and also to the overloading of the aircraft beyond the weight at which it could be safely flown on one engine only. Almost immediately after the Marauder had entered service, it had been found necessary to add more and more equipment, armament, fuel and armour, driving the gross weight steadily upwards. By early 1942, the B-26 had risen in normal gross weight from its original 26,625 lb to 31,527 lb with no increase in power. It had been found that many of the accidents had been caused by engine failures, which were in turn caused by a combination of poor maintenance by relatively inexperienced mechanics and a change from 100 octane fuel to 100 octane aromatic fuel, which damaged the diaphragm of the carburettors. Many of the B-26 instructors were almost as inexperienced as the pilots they were trying to train, and did not know themselves how to handle the B-26 in asymmetric configuration – in other words, on one engine only. Consequently, they were in no position to pass on the necessary technique to their pupils.

Doolittle sent his technical adviser, Captain Vincent W. "Squeak" Burnett, to make a tour of OTU (Operational Training Units) bases to demonstrate how the B-26 could be flown safely. These demonstrations included single-engine operations, slow-flying characteristics, and recoveries from unusual flight attitudes. Captain Burnett made numerous low-altitude flights with one engine out, even turning into a dead engine (which aircrews were warned never to do), proving that the Marauder could be safely flown if you knew what you were doing. Martin also sent engineers out into the field to show crews how to avoid problems caused by overloading, by paying proper attention to the aircraft's centre of gravity.

The efforts of the Army and the Martin Company to improve training soon began to pay dividends. Within a few weeks B-26 accidents at the training establishments had been reduced to about the same level as that experienced by other combat types. Despite this, inevitable rumours persisted that the B-26 was a death trap, and new crews were extremely wary of it. It took the Marauder's prowess in action to prove that it was, in fact, a superb fighting machine. It excelled itself in New Guinea, making fast, low-level attacks on Japanese airfields and installations that left the enemy dazed and bewildered.

The original operational Marauder group, the 22nd BG, used B-26s exclusively until October 1943, when some B-25s were added. In February 1944 it became a heavy bombardment group, equipped with B-24s. The next variant, the B-26B, had uprated engines and increased armament. Of the 1883 built, all but the first 641 aircraft featured a new extended-span wing and taller tail fin.

The B-26B made its debut in the European Theatre with the 322nd BG in March 1943. After some disastrous low-level daylight attacks, all B-26 units in the European Theatre were reassigned to the medium-level bombing role. They fulfilled this role magnificently until the end of the war in both north-west Europe and Italy. The B-26C, of which 1210 were built, was essentially similar to the later

B-26B models. These were succeeded by the B-26F (300 built), in which the angle of incidence (i.e. the angle at which the wing is married to the fuselage) was increased in order to improve take-off performance. The final model was the B-26G, which differed from the F model in only minor detail; 950 were built.

The B-26 saw service in the Aleutians in 1942, and in the Western Desert, where it served with the RAF Middle East Command as the Marauder Mk I (B-26A), Marauder Mk IA (B-26B), Marauder Mk II (B-26F) and Marauder Mk III (B-26G). Only two RAF squadrons, Nos 14 and 39, used the Marauder. The total number of Marauders delivered to the RAF included 52 Marauder Mk Is and Mk IAs, 250 Marauder Mk IIs and 150 Marauder Mk IIIs. The Marauder was also used extensively by the Free French Air Force and the South African Air Force. Many Marauders were completed or converted as AT-23 or TB-26 trainers for the USAAF and JM-1s for the US Navy, some being used as target tugs. Production totalled 5175 aircraft.

CHAPTER EIGHT

One-Way Mission: Germany's Suicide Aircraft

I n March 1942 the *Luftwaffe* formed a special duties unit, designated KG 200, to meet an *Abwehr* (German Military Intelligence Service) requirement for a clandestine flying unit equipped with aircraft that would be capable of landing supplies and saboteurs at any point within the European theatre of operations. I/KG 200's operations were carried out under the direct orders of the *Gestapo*, the *Sicherheitsdienst* (Security Service, or SD) and the *Abwehr*, and many of its missions were undertaken with complete success. The *Gruppe's* more spectacular operations included flying a party of *Abwehr* and SD agents into Persia (Iran) to carry out an underground offensive against Allied stores and supply dumps as well as to set up a pro-German supply and intelligence network in the area, and dropping a team of commandos into Russia with orders to kill Stalin.

During most of its operational career up to 1944, KG 200 was commanded by *Oberst* Heigl, who, in the spring of that year, became involved in a bizarre special operation – the formation of a German suicide squadron. Throughout the operational planning and testing phase, the whole suicide squadron came under the administrative control of KG 200.

The idea of forming a suicide squadron was originally conceived in early 1943 by one of Heigl's subordinates, *Hauptmann* Heinrich Lange. Before taking the scheme to higher authority, Lange set about recruiting a band of colleagues, all of whom shared similar opinions to his own and all of whom were prepared to lay down their lives without hesitation if it meant Germany's salvation. Some of the volunteers were glider pilots who had never flown a powered aircraft, but they were confident that they could handle a machine on its one-way suicide trip.

The person chosen to present the scheme to higher authority was the famous woman aviator Hannah Reitsch, who already enjoyed the confidence of most senior *Luftwaffe* officers. The full support of the *Luftwaffe* had to be obtained before the idea could be presented to Hitler, who would have to give the final seal of approval. Reitsch found obstacles in her path right from the outset. Officials thought the idea preposterous and refused to take her seriously. Only after considerable persistence did she succeed in meeting *Feldmarschall* Erhard Milch, the senior officer responsible for the *Luftwaffe* equipment programme in the German Air Ministry. Milch said the scheme was ridiculous, impracticable and obviously the idea of a few fanatics who were tired of life and who wished to secure a place as martyrs in German folklore. In the end, he gave his reluctant promise to see what he could do, but Hannah Reitsch left his office convinced that the matter would end there and that Milch was hoping that the idea would fade away.

Several weeks passed and nothing happened. Finally, Reitsch decided to bypass Milch and approach the German Academy of Aeronautics. This organisation would ultimately be responsible for providing the team of scientists and engineers necessary to bring the scheme to fruition. Professor Dr Walter Georgii, Director of the German Aeronautical Research Council, expressed an interest in the project and called a meeting with representatives of the suicide group to discuss the details. The conference went on for two days and was often stormy, but it was decided by a narrow margin that the plan was feasible and would go ahead.

One of the factors that influenced this decision was that a suitable aircraft already existed. This was the Messerschmitt Me 328, a tiny wooden aircraft powered by Argus As 014 impulse ducts similar to those used on the V-1 flying bomb. Cheap and easy to manufacture, the Me 328 came as close as possible to the ideal aircraft for the kind of operation envisaged, and its use would mean that no valuable time would be wasted in developing an aircraft specifically for the task. The Me 328 had originally been conceived by Messerschmitt Flugzeugbau towards the end of 1942 as a high-speed bomber that could also be used in the day-fighter role, but as time went by it

The Me 328 was an ideal design for the suicide mission. Cheap and simple to construct, it could be handled by inexperienced pilots.

became obvious that because of its low cost and simplicity of production it would be better suited for use as flying artillery against heavily defended land targets and ships. The aircraft's high speed meant that the pilot need not worry too much about the risk of interception by Allied fighters at low level, and its small size would make it a difficult target for anti-aircraft defences. The idea was that the pilot would aim his machine carefully at the target, then bale out in the seconds before impact.

In March 1943, development of the Me 328 was handed over to the Jacob Schweyer Glider Manufacturing Co., which worked in conjunction with Messerschmitt and the *Deutsche Forschungsanstalt für Segelflug*, the German Research Institute for Glider Flight. Development work was carried out on two separate variants, the Me 328A interceptor, which was designed to attack American daylight bomber formations, and the Me 328B low-level bomber. An early problem was the positioning of the impulse ducts; in the original design these were to have been attached by struts on each side of the fuselage aft of the trailing edge, exhausting under the tailplane. However, this configuration was found to be unsatisfactory because of the power plant's high vibration level. Instead, it was decided to mount the units on the wing. In the end, the ducts were slung at quarter span, the intakes a foot aft of the wing leading edges.

The first test airframes were completed by Jacob Schweyer as pure gliders without power plants, and one of these was mounted on a rig above the fuselage of a Dornier Do 217E for flight tests. The first trials were carried out at Horsching, near Linz in Austria. The

Me 328 was released at altitudes between 9000 and 18,000 feet, and manoeuvres were performed throughout the airframe's full speed range of between 90 and 460 mph. During these tests the aircraft displayed poor handling characteristics, but was thought to be sufficiently capable for its intended mission.

Soon after flight testing began, work on the Me 328A was abandoned and development concentrated on the Me 328B. The aircraft's diminutive fuselage, whose maximum diameter was only 3 ft 11 in, was occupied almost completely by self-sealing fuel tanks, two in the nose and two in the rear fuselage, each holding 110 gallons. The two nose tanks were separated by a 15 mm armoured bulkhead, while the pilot was protected by 15 mm armour plate positioned in front of the cockpit and an 80 mm bullet-proof windscreen. An additional space beneath the pilot's seat could be used to accommodate either extra fuel or anti-personnel bombs. There were balloon cable cutters in the nose and along the entire leading edges of the wings, which had a span of 22 ft 7 in. The Argus As 014 impulse duct tubes were flexibly mounted under the wings, the under surface being protected from the heat by layers of asbestos. The Me 328B took off on a jettisonable undercarriage, and for landing there was a retractable skid of composite wood and steel construction recessed into the fuselage. The rack for the aircraft's 2200 lb bomb was attached to this skid.

More problems arose when flight testing began with the Argus tubes fitted, and there were several accidents resulting from structural failure caused by the heavy vibration from the power plants. The two Argus pulse ducts produced 880 lb of thrust each, giving the Me 328B a maximum speed of 502 mph at sea level and 453 mph at 9800 feet in a clean configuration. With a 2200 lb bomb the maximum speed was reduced to 391 mph at sea level and 283 mph at altitude. The aircraft's ceiling with a 2200 lb bomb was 9200 feet and the range was 345 miles. In its suicide role it was envisaged that the Me 328B would be adapted to carry a 2000 lb bomb-torpedo in the nose.

On anti-shipping operations the pilot would be expected to steer the aircraft into the water at a shallow angle, when the airframe would break up. The impact would automatically start a time fuse and the bomb would continue under the water to explode under the keel of the target vessel. Because of the unsatisfactory record of the Me 328's pulse jets during flight testing, the aircraft was to be used as a glider in this suicide role. It would be carried to the neighbourhood of the target on the back of a Dornier Do 217E. Once within gliding range of the objective, the pilot would release himself from the mother aircraft and glide to the attack at 455 mph at a gliding angle of 12:1.

Early in 1944, while flight testing of the Me 328 continued, the suicide volunteer group judged that the time was ripe to place the project before Hitler. Hannah Reitsch was summoned to Hitler's mountain retreat at Berchtesgaden on 28 February 1944. For three hours Hitler and his *Luftwaffe* adjutant, *Oberst* von Below, listened as she went into the scheme in great detail. The conference was only a partial success. Hitler objected to the suicide idea on the grounds that it was without precedent in German history. Hannah Reitsch's argument was that Germany was now in greater danger than ever before, and the situation called for revolutionary and untried methods. She managed to secure the *Führer*'s permission to allow development work to continue, but he emphasised that an operation of the type envisaged could only be carried out in the event of dire extremity, and only at his own express command.

The interview did not produce the result that the volunteers had hoped for, but at least Hitler had not rejected the scheme outright. His approval for development work to continue also now opened many hitherto closed doors. One door led to General Korton, head of the *Luftwaffe* General Staff, later to die in the bomb plot against Hitler's life on 20 July 1944. Although Korton was not enthusiastic about the project, he could not ignore the fact that Hitler had given his partial blessing to it, and he promised as much assistance as possible. Korton placed the project under the control of *Oberst* Heigl and KG 200.

By the time Heigl assumed his appointment in March 1944, the group numbered more than seventy volunteers. There was no need for an open recruiting drive: the word soon spread about the group's activities and there was a steady stream of applications to join it. The vetting of potential recruits was very strict, and new members were only accepted after undergoing extensive psychological tests designed to establish whether they would measure up to their task when the time came. Each would-be suicide pilot signed a pledge that read: 'I hereby volunteer as a pilot of the manned glider bomb. I am aware that this action will end with my death'.

The project was now under the direct control of the *Reichsluftministerium* and technical development was supervised by a team of engineers led by Heinz Kensche, a glider expert. Kensche selected Hannah Reitsch to flight test the Me 328 and be in overall charge of the volunteers' flying training on the type as soon as the flight test programme was complete. The Me 328 was ordered into quantity production in April 1944 and everything appeared set for the working up of the suicide group into an operational *Luftwaffe* unit. Then a whole spate of difficulties cropped up, many of which still remain unexplained; they included problems in releasing the Me 328 from its Dornier Do 217 parent aircraft. Lengthy delays in production plans led Hannah Reitsch and her colleagues to suspect that there was an official move afoot to delay the suicide project or bring it to a halt altogether.

When it became apparent that there would be a delay of several months before the Me 328 was ready for operations, the group began to look around for another aircraft type that would fill the gap and be ready in time to repel an Allied invasion. After hurried consultation, the type selected was a manned version of the Fieseler Fi 103 (V-1) flying bomb, also known as the FZG 76. Work on modifying the V-1 to carry a pilot began almost immediately, the project proceeding under the code name 'Reichenberg'. Its true nature was kept highly secret, so that even the engineers directly involved with it believed that the piloted V-1 was intended to be flight tested to solve some problems experienced in the aerodynamic performance of the V-1 flying bomb itself. The modification programme was supervised by Dr Lusser of the Fielder Construction Bureau located at the Henschel factory in Berlin-Schönfeld.

The design team produced four variants of the piloted V-1 in a fortnight, the only changes to the basic airframe being the installation of a cockpit just forward of the Argus As 014 impulse duct, and the fitting of ailerons to the flying bomb's wing. The first prototype, the Reichenberg I, was completed as a glider and was fitted with landing skids, its purpose being to familiarise the future instructors with the aircraft's aerodynamic characteristics. A two-seat version with dual controls was to be used as a trainer. The Reichenberg II was also a trainer, but this version was fitted with a power unit as well as the landing skids. The operational version was the Reichenberg III, which was fitted with a 1780lb warhead in the nose. Its maximum speed and range were 360 mph and 150 miles.

Hannah Reitsch's requests to be allowed to pilot the V-1 herself were at first turned down and two pilots from the *Luftwaffe* flight test centre at Rechlin were selected for the task. Both crashed and were seriously injured on their second flight, at which point Reitsch

The piloted version of the V-1 flying bomb, the Reichenberg IV, would undoubtedly have caused damage to the Allied invasion fleet.

was called in to supervise the test programme. Soon afterwards, she herself was injured in a crash-landing and replaced by *Leutnant* Starbati, who was killed in one of the early test flights. Starbati in turn was replaced by a *Feldwebel* Schenk who was also killed in the test programme. Heinz Kensche, the suicide group's engineer, also took part in the testing and he narrowly escaped being killed when his V-1 went out of control due to excessive vibrations at low altitude. He managed to bale out just in time. Extensive tests showed that these accidents had been caused by excessive vibrations set up by the 740 lb thrust of the Argus 014 engine operating under full power, which also explained why one-third of all V-1 flying bombs launched against southern England failed to reach their targets because of mechanical failure.

Nevertheless, despite the risks involved and the high casualty rate, it was decided that the piloted V-1 would be suitable for the suicide group's task. It was argued that the average *Luftwaffe* pilot would be able to handle the machine satisfactorily in the air, and although considerable danger was involved in landing the machine, this would hardly be important on a suicide trip. During the training programme, landings were only to be carried out in the two-seat version under strict dual instruction by qualified instructors.

During the powered trials, the Reichenberg was carried by a Heinkel He 111 mother aircraft, slung underneath the starboard wing between the engine and fuselage. The Reichenberg pilot kept in touch with the Heinkel crew by means of a throat microphone, over which he issued instructions for the release. The extremely tricky landing was made 'power off' at speeds varying between 53 and 133 mph, depending on the aircraft's angle of descent. This was high without power and the safe technique was to fly the aircraft straight on with no attempt at rounding out. In the latter event the V-1 sank like a stone, and damage almost invariably resulted.

Despite all the hazards a nucleus of pilots had been trained by the beginning of June 1944; attack plans for use against Allied shipping had been drawn up and operational training initiated. The target ship was simulated by coloured smoke bombs released at 6500 feet, allowing the pilot of the V-1 to make approaches to the smoke cloud to experiment with angles and speeds. An aiming device was also developed, consisting of a graduated celluloid plate that enabled the pilot to compute the draught of the vessel (depth below the surface) and indicate how far from the ship the V-1 would have to crash into the water in order to allow the torpedo to pass beneath the keel of the vessel, where it was to explode by means of the time fuse. To determine the point at which the V-1 had to hit the water relative to the ship, the size and weight of the vessel had to be determined as closely as possible; the pilot would then enter this information on a slide rule on his angle-of-dive indicator, enabling him to select the correct angle and maintain it from the moment he chose his target until the V-1 hit the water. It therefore followed that pilots had to familiarise themselves with the characteristics and tonnages of major Allied vessels. The final approach to the target was to be made at such a high speed that anti-aircraft fire would have little chance of engaging the V-1. During the flight trials, Reitsch and other pilots tested the machine in dives at speeds of more than 520 mph.

On 6 June 1944, while training was still in progress, the Allied invasion forces stormed ashore in Normandy, robbing the whole suicide project of much of the reason for its existence. With the firm establishment of the Allied beachheads on the Continent, there was no longer any possibility that the suicide volunteers could change the course of the war by their deaths, and enthusiasm for the scheme rapidly began to wane. Several new projects were put forward, including the use of the volunteer group on suicide missions against targets on the eastern front, using conventional aircraft such as the Focke-Wulf Fw 190 carrying a 4000 lb bomb. The volunteers, however, believed that nothing could be achieved by sacrificing themselves uselessly against some ammunition dump on the Russian front, and there was general relief when Hitler personally forbade the use of the Fw 190 in this role.

The suggestion had in fact been Heigl's. As a result, he was openly rebuked by Hitler and replaced as commanding officer of KG 200 by *Oberstleutnant* Werner Baumbach, a highly popular officer who had proved himself many times in combat. Under his direction, the suicide idea took on a new lease of life and the technical development and construction of the Me 328 and the piloted version of the V-1, 175 of which were completed in the assembly plant at Dannenberg, continued in February and March 1945. It was only terminated in early April, a month before the collapse of Germany.

CHAPTER NINE

Japan's 'Flaming Coffins'

On 10 December 1941, just three days after the devastating attack on the US Pacific Fleet at Pearl Harbor, Japanese aircraft dealt a further serious blow to Allied naval power in the Far East. A mixed force of Japanese bombers and torpedo-bombers sank the British battleship HMS *Prince of Wales* and the battlecruiser HMS *Repulse* off the coast of Malaya.

One of the principal Japanese bomber types involved in this attack was the Mitsubishi G4M1, later to be known to the Allies by the code name 'Betty'. First flown in October 1939, the G4M1 was developed to a specification that demanded extremely long range, even if this meant packing as much fuel as possible into the wings by dispensing with such things as armour plating for the crew and vital components, and self-sealing protection for the fuel tanks. The result was an aircraft with an almost unheard-of long-range performance, whose crews could expect an extremely unpleasant death if their aircraft were set on fire, especially since few Japanese aircrew carried parachutes, at least in the early days of the Pacific war.

The G4M1 was conceived in 1938 as a replacement for the Mitsubishi G3M (Type 96) series of bombers, which dated back to 1934 and had been widely used during the Sino-Japanese wars of the 1930s. The Imperial Japanese Navy (IJN) demanded a bomber with a maximum range of 2600 nautical miles without a weapons load, and 2000 nautical miles with a 1760 lb torpedo or equivalent bomb load. Although Mitsubishi proposed a four-engined aircraft to meet these requirements, the IJN insisted on a twin-engined design. To achieve the range requirements, it was necessary to carry 1100 gallons of fuel in completely unprotected wing tanks, as the use of protected tanks would have reduced the bomber's range by 45 per cent.

Designed by a team under the leadership of Kiro Honjo, the G4M1, or Type 1 Model 11, was issued to the IJN in April 1941, beginning its operational career in May with attacks on Chungking and Chengtu in south-east China. At the beginning of the Pacific war, 120 G4M1s were in service with the IJN, all with the *Kanoya Kokutai* (Air Corps) on Formosa. Early in December 1941, twenty-seven G4M1s were transferred to French Indo-China to strengthen the force earmarked to take part in the assault on Malaya; the remaining ninety-three were retained on Formosa for operations against Allied forces in the Philippines, where they encountered only minimal opposition. After operations in the Dutch East Indies, New Guinea and the Solomons, G4M1 bombers joined Japanese carrier aircraft in attacks on Darwin and other targets in northern Australia, the first of these taking place on 19 February 1942.

Up to this time the G4M1, nicknamed *Hamaki* (Cigar) because of the shape of its fuselage, had escaped relatively unscathed, having encountered second-rate anti-aircraft defences. However, in the attacks on Australia its vulnerability began to show, even though the defending Allied fighters were outclassed by the escorting Mitsubishi A6M Zero fighters. Most of these attacks were made at high and medium level. However, a few months later, during the battle for Guadalcanal, G4M1s flying from Rabaul attempted to attack US transports from a relatively low altitude and were decimated. On 8 August 1942, seventeen out of twenty-six G4M1s were destroyed by anti-aircraft fire and US fighters; one aircraft crashed into the US transport George F. Elliott, which caught fire and had to be abandoned.

In an attempt to rectify at least some of the problems, Mitsubishi developed the Navy Type 1 Attack Bomber Model 12. This aircraft, which retained the short designation G4M1, was powered by two Kasei 15 engines, which developed increased power ratings at altitude, enabling the aircraft to fly above the effective ceiling of light anti-aircraft guns. The lateral 7.7 mm gun blisters were exchanged for glazed flush panels, and the shape of the tail cone, housing a flexible 20 mm cannon, was altered. Losses decreased somewhat, but only at the expense of an increased gross weight and a reduction in performance, including a loss of about 200 nautical miles in range.

The G4M1 operated throughout the six months of the Guadalcanal campaign, continuing to suffer heavy losses but also making effective night attacks, especially by the torpedo-bombers. On the night of 29/30 January 1943, for example, G4M1s severely damaged the heavy cruiser USS *Chicago*, which was sunk in a second attack. Two other cruisers, the *Wichita* and *Louisville*, were also torpedoed, but the torpedoes failed to explode. In addition, the destroyer *La Valette* was torpedoed, but survived.

It was during the final stages of the Solomon Islands campaign that the 'Betty' suffered a much-publicised loss. On 18 April 1943 Lockheed P-38 Lightnings of the 339th Fighter Squadron, USAAF, shot down a G4M bomber carrying Admiral Isoroku Yamamoto, the IJN Commander-in-Chief. To do the job, the Lightnings made an 1100-mile round trip from Guadalcanal to intercept Yamamoto's aircraft over Kahili Atoll. The bomber (together with a second, carrying Yamamoto's staff) was escorted by six Zeros of Air Group 204 from Rabaul, led by Lieutenant Takeshi. One reason for the comparatively light escort was that the Japanese command at Rabaul did not believe that any US aircraft could present a threat at such a range; the Japanese were also unaware that the Americans had deciphered their Navy code, so that the exact timing of Yamamoto's flight was known.

The vulnerability of the G4M was underlined by Japanese air operations against northern Australia, where the bomber's losses mounted as the air defence grew increasingly determined. Throughout 1942, the air defence of northern Australia was the responsibility of the 49th Fighter Group, USAAF (equipped with P-40E Kittyhawks), which was joined after August by Nos 76 and 77 Squadrons RAAF, also armed with this type. As the P-40 was no match for the Zero, the Australian government urgently requested a shipment of Spitfires from the UK. Following a lengthy delay, three Spitfire squadrons – No. 54 RAF and Nos 452 and 457 RAAF – were established in the Darwin area in mid-January 1943, together with their radar-equipped Mobile Fighter Sector HQ. The three squadrons formed No. 1 Fighter Wing, which was led by Wing Commander Clive Caldwell, a highly experienced and skilled fighter pilot with twenty victories to his credit in North Africa.

In February 1943 the Japanese renewed their bombing offensive against northern Australia, and on the 6th of that month Flight Lieutenant R.W. Foster opened the Spitfire's scoreboard in the theatre by shooting down a Mitsubishi Ki-46 'Dinah' reconnaissance aircraft 35 miles WNW of Cape Van Dieman. It was

A Japanese airfield under attack by an RAAF Beaufighter. Japanese aircraft burned just as readily on the ground as they did in the air.

a good start, because so far the 'Dinahs had been able to operate with virtual impunity, their speed and ceiling making them virtually immune to interception by fighters such as the P-40. The arrival of the Spitfire – and the Lockheed P-38F, which was now being deployed by the Americans – now changed that situation. It remained to be seen how the tropicalised Spitfire VC would perform against the Zero. The pilots were confident that whatever performance shortcomings the Spitfire might have when confronted by the Japanese fighter – and by now the Allies knew just how well the A6M performed – they would be levelled out by superior skill and tactics. This confidence seemed to be justified when, during a raid on Coomalie by sixteen Nakajima B5N 'Kate' torpedo-bombers with a fighter escort on 2 March, the Spitfires claimed two Zeros and a 'Kate' for no loss. On 23 March Darwin was subjected to its fifty-third air attack, during which twenty-one bombers and twenty-four escorting Zeros were intercepted by the whole of No. 1 Fighter Wing. In the air battle that developed over the harbour, the Spitfires shot down three Zeros and four G4M 'Betty' bombers, but three Spitfires were lost.

There were no raids on the Darwin area in April 1943, but at 0926 hours on Sunday 2 May, an incoming Japanese force was detected by radar while it was still a long way out to sea – 49 minutes' flying time from the coast, in fact. The Wing's thirty-three Spitfires were all airborne within 15 minutes. The enemy formation, comprising eighteen bombers and twenty-seven fighters, was sighted when the Spitfires were at 23,000 ft (7000m). Since the Japanese were still about 4000 ft higher up, Caldwell knew that to attack them on the climb would be suicidal, for the nimble Zeros would have all the advantages. He therefore delayed and continued to climb while the . Spitfires got into position above the enemy, with the glare of the sun behind them. At 1015 hours the Japanese flew over Darwin and bombed the harbour unmolested, while the Spitfires were still trying to get into position. After completing their bombing run the enemy altered course and crossed the coast, losing height gradually as they increased speed. The Spitfires were now at 32,000 feet behind the Japanese formation.

Caldwell's fighters shadowed the Japanese until they were out over the Timor Sea, then he ordered No. 54 Squadron to attack the Zeros while the other two squadrons engaged the bombers. The Spitfires, now with the advantage of height, went into the attack almost vertically at 400 mph. A furious air battle developed as the Zero pilots, recovering from their surprise, turned to meet the attackers. It was now that the Spitfire pilots learned a bitter lesson. The lightly built Zero, with its high power-weight ratio, could out-turn the Spitfire VC with ease. It could also perform some extraordinary manoeuvres that the pilot of anything but a Zero would never dare attempt in the middle of a dogfight. For example, one experienced Australian pilot was making a shallow diving attack on a Zero when the enemy fighter suddenly performed a tight loop that brought it on to the tail of the Australian, who narrowly avoided being shot down. When the battle was over, five Zeros had been shot down, but only one bomber; and on the debit side five Spitfires had been lost in combat, two of the pilots being killed, while five more had to make emergency landings because of fuel starvation and another three because of engine failure. The Australian popular press was scathing in its criticism.

By the end of May 1943, No. 1 Fighter Wing had destroyed twenty-four enemy aircraft for the loss of ten Spitfires in combat. Other Spitfires, though, were lost in forced landings; the Merlin engines were suffering badly from wear and tear, and replacements were non-existent. During high-altitude actions problems were experienced with the Spitfires' 20 mm cannon, the freezing conditions causing malfunction and jamming. Even if only one cannon jammed, the recoil from the other caused the aircraft to yaw so that the aim was spoiled.

Ignoring the growing storm of criticism about the famous Spitfire's lack of success, Caldwell continued to refine the fighter wing's tactics, confident that the situation was about to change. It did, on 20 June 1943. That morning, Darwin radar detected enemy aircraft approaching, and within minutes forty-six Spitfires were airborne. A short time later, the pilots of Nos 54 and 452 Squadrons, climbing hard, sighted twenty-five Japanese bombers over Bathurst Island, escorted by a similar number of Zeros. The enemy, at 28,000ft, were slightly lower than the two Spitfire squadrons, which immediately launched their attack. No. 54 Squadron destroyed seven G4M bombers and a Zero, while No. 452 Squadron shot down three G4Ms and one fighter. The enemy formation altered course towards Darwin, where No. 457 Squadron shot down a 'Betty'. After releasing their bombs, the enemy flew across Darwin harbour, losing another two Zeros. Meanwhile, ten more bombers had made a low-level attack on Darwin airfield without fighter opposition, but as they withdrew they were intercepted by No. 54 Squadron, which destroyed another bomber. During the morning's engagements the fighter wing lost only two Spitfires, both of No. 452 Squadron. Against twelve bombers and four fighters destroyed, it was not a bad balance sheet. For once, the critics were silenced.

On 30 June twenty-seven 'Bettys' escorted by twenty-three Zeros attacked Long and Fenton airfields, from where US Fifth Air Force B-24 bombers had just begun a series of heavy attacks on Japanese bases in the Celebes. In the course of a running battle with the Spitfires, the Japanese lost six 'Bettys' and three Zeros; four Spitfires were written off, three as a result of engine failure. By now, the Spitfires' engines were so worn out that when the fighter wing put up thirty-six aircraft to intercept forty-seven Japanese bombers and fighters, only seven managed to engage the enemy. Nevertheless, the seven that did engage, with superb tactical skill, destroyed seven 'Bettys' and two Zeros. Once the fighter escort had been overcome, the Spitfire pilots were finding the fuel-laden G4Ms easy prey.

Night attacks by 'Betty' torpedo-bombers on Allied naval forces continued throughout 1943, and caused serious concern, one of the problems being that the US Navy had no dedicated night fighters. Early night fighting in the US Navy, like its land-based counterpart, was an improvised business. It had its beginnings in November 1943, when six heavy and five light carriers of the US Navy's Task Force 50 opened the campaign to capture the Gilbert Island with a two-day series of strikes on Japanese airfields and installations in support of American landings on the Tarawa and Makin Atolls.

The task force commander, Rear-Admiral Pownall, was concerned about Japanese night attacks on his ships, and invited suggestions on how they might be protected. Lieutenant-Commander Edward H. (Butch) O'Hare, commanding Air Group 6 on the carrier USS *Enterprise*, and some of his fellow pilots came up with a possible answer. The USS *Enterprise* had one of the new radar-equipped Grumman TBF-1C Avengers, and the plan was to form an interception team with this aircraft and two Grumman F6F Hellcat fighters. The Hellcats, each of which would be flown by a pilot with night experience, would form up on the Avenger; the formation would be vectored to the vicinity of an enemy contact by the carrier's fighter director and the Avenger's radar would then take over, bringing the fighters to within visual range of the target.

The first sortie, on the night of 24/25 November, did not result in any intercepts, but on the night of 26/27 the trio got in amongst a formation of G4M bombers and caused havoc. The Avenger was the aircraft that scored, its pilot and gunner accounting for two of the 'Bettys'; the Wildcats also attacked separate targets, with the result that the enemy raid was severely disrupted. Butch O'Hare went missing during this engagement and was never seen again.

As new American fighter types such as the Grumman F6F Hellcat arrived in the Pacific, the Japanese began to suffer combat losses that were little short of staggering. The US pilots, now skilfully led by veterans with two years of experience behind them, rapidly assumed a superiority that would never be lost, gaining formidable successes in dogfights that were often unbelievably one-sided. In 1944, it was the Hellcat that ruled the Pacific sky, its superiority culminating in in the massive air battle that was to go down in history as the 'Great Marianas Turkey Shoot'. It happened in June 1944, during the Battle of the Philippine Sea, when waves of Japanese aircraft attacked the US task force that was undertaking a major amphibious operation to occupy key objectives in the Marianas.

On 19 June, with the amphibious invasion in full swing, large numbers of Japanese bombers and torpedo-bombers made a series of desperate attempts to hit the task force; they were detected by radar at a range of 150 miles, and the carrier fighters were waiting for them. The agile Hellcats swarmed all over the attackers before they even sighted the carriers, and of the 200 Japanese aircraft in the first two strike waves, only 30 escaped. At the close of the day, the Japanese had lost a staggering 402 aircraft. G4Ms featured prominently in this operation, shot down in flames as they tried to press home suicidal torpedo attacks.

Variants of the basic G4M1 design included the much-improved G4M2, which made its appearance in November 1941; this variant gradually replaced the G4M1, which was assigned to transport, reconnaissance and training duties. Sub-variants of the G4M2 were the G4M2a, with Kasei 25 engines; the high-altitude G4M2b, with Kasei 27s; the G4M2c (Kasei 25b engines); and the G4M2d, which was a turbojet engine test bed. The G4M2e was specially modified to carry the Yokosuka Ohka (Cherry Blossom) piloted suicide aircraft. Incredibly, no attempt to rectify the 'Betty's' principal shortcomings – lack of armour and lack of fuel tank protection – was made until 1944 with the last bomber version, the G4M3, but only 60 were completed out of a total production figure of 2479.

One of the last tasks of the G4M before the end of the Pacific war was to act as carrier aircraft for the Yokosuka Ohka rocket-powered suicide missile. The notion of a pilot deliberately sacrificing his life as an act of war was foreign to western minds in the Second World War, but the Japanese brought the concept to grim reality in their Special Attack Corps, whose ultimate development was the Ohka suicide bomb. One of the more sinister weapons to emerge from the Second World War, the unpowered prototype MXY7 Ohka suicide aircraft first flew in October 1944 and was followed by forty-five examples of the Ohka K-1 training model, which was also unpowered. The production model was the Ohka Model 11, of which 755 were built between September 1944 and March 1945.

The Ohka went into action for the first time on 21 March 1945, but the sixteen Mitsubishi G4M2e parent aircraft (which carried the Ohkas shackled under the open bomb bay) were intercepted and forced to release their bombs short of the target. The first success came on 1 April, when Ohkas damaged the battleship *West Virginia* and three transport vessels. The first ship to be destroyed by an Ohka was the destroyer *Mannert L. Abele*, lost off Okinawa on 12 April. Several versions of the Ohka were proposed, including the turbojet-powered Model 33, but none materialised in operational form before the end of the war. The concept of the Ohka was sound enough, but it suffered from a lack of suitable carrier aircraft, which consistently failed to break through the Allied fighter screen. A long-range version, and one intended to be catapulted from a surfaced submarine, were under development when the war ended.

Every Japanese aircraft type, including the celebrated A6M Zero, was vulnerable because of a lack of armour protection. In order to meet the exacting Navy requirements, weight conservation was of paramount importance, and the Zero design featured several innovations in order to achieve this goal. For example, the wing was built in one piece, eliminating the need for the heavy centre-section fittings that were normally required to join two separate wing sections together. The one-piece wing combined with the engine, cockpit and forward fuselage to form a single rigid unit, the centre section of the fuselage being riveted to the upper wing skin, the latter forming the cockpit floor. The rear fuselage, with the tail, was joined to the forward section by a series of eighty bolts, fixed to two ring formers just aft of the cockpit. The aircraft could therefore readily be split into two components, facilitating storage and also providing unobstructed access to the cockpit area from the rear. Another weight-saving device was the use of a lightweight alloy called Extra-Super Duralumin (ESD) in the construction of the wing main spar. Manufactured by the Sumitomo Metal Industry, it had a tensile strength 30 to 40 per cent higher than any alloy used previously. Although very light in weight (3704 lb empty, compared with the Spitfire I's 4341 lb), a feature that gave the impression that the airframe was structurally weak, the Zero fighter design was actually very strong. The overall result was a light and highly manoeuvrable aircraft fitted with a very powerful engine.

For the first eighteen months of the Pacific war, when the Zero encountered aircraft types over which it was always superior, its power margin and high manoeuvrability brought it massive success. From 1943 it met its match in the F6F Hellcat and other types, and now its lack of protection resulted in unacceptable losses; a single well-aimed burst from a Hellcat's six 0.50 in machine-guns was usually enough to set a Zero ablaze.

It was not until the appearance of the A6M5b sub-variant in 1944 that the Japanese at last woke up to the fact that protection, both for the pilot and for vital parts of the aircraft, was an all-important factor in combat survival. This sub-variant, which was jointly developed by Mitsubishi and Dai-Ichi Kaigun Kokusho, featured an automatic CO_2 fire extinguisher system built into the fuel tank areas of the fuselage and around the engine firewall, while a 2 in bullet-proof windshield was fitted to give the pilot some forward protection. Thanks to the extraordinary Japanese mentality that continued to prevail at the time, there was still no rear protection for the pilot; the notion that a Japanese pilot might need to run away from an adversary was inconceivable. Firepower was also increased in the A6M5b, one of the two fuselage-mounted 7.7 mm machine-guns being replaced by a heavier 13 mm weapon. Despite these improvements, IJN fighter units equipped with the A6M5 (which were the majority) suffered massive losses during the battle for the Philippines in the latter half of 1944. Many of the A6M5s were fitted with a 550 lb bomb and expended in *kamikaze* attacks.

CHAPTER TEN

The Messerschmitt Me 163 Komet: Revolutionary and Deadly

On 28 July 1944, P-51 Mustangs of the US Eighth Army Air Force's 359th Fighter Group, led by Colonel Avelin P. Tacon, Jr, were escorting B-17s at 25,000 feet over Merseburg when the pilots sighted two condensation trails at six o'clock, five miles astern and several thousand feet higher up. The Mustang leader's combat report described the ensuing action:

I identified them immediately as the new jet-propelled aircraft. Their contrails could not be mistaken and looked very dense and white, somewhat like an elongated cumulus cloud some three-quarters of a mile in length. My section turned 180 degrees back towards the enemy, which included two with jets turned on and three in a glide without jets operating at the moment. The two I had spotted made a diving turn to the left in close formation and feinted towards the bombers at six o'clock, cutting off their jets as they turned. Our flight turned for a head-on pass to get between them and the rear of the bomber formation. While still 3000 yards from the bombers, they turned into us and left the bombers alone. In this turn they banked about 80 degrees but their course changed only about 20 degrees. Their turn radius was very large but their rate of roll appeared excellent. Their speed, I estimated, was 500 to 600 mph. Both planes passed under us 1000 feet below while still in a close formation glide. In an attempt to follow them, I split-Sd. One continued down in a 45-degree dive, the other climbed up into the sun very steeply and I lost him. Then I looked back at the one in the dive and saw he was five miles away at 10,000 feet.

In fact, the attackers were not jet aircraft at all, but early operational examples of the rocket-powered Messerschmitt Me 163 *Komet*. This remarkable little aircraft was based on the experimental DFS 194 tailless aircraft, designed in 1938 by Dr Alexander Lippisch.

The DFS 194 was the culmination of Lippisch's long involvement with tailless aircraft. His interest had begun in 1926, when he designed a tailless glider named the *Storch* (Stork). Subsequent variants were fitted with small engines, and in 1933 Lippisch and his design team were installed at the Sailplane Research Establishment (DFS) at Darmstadt, where their experiments continued. In 1937, Lippisch received an RLM order for the construction of a rocket-powered tailless aircraft, the DFS 39, which was to have been built jointly by DFS and Heinkel. However, Heinkel was preoccupied with its first turbojet aircraft, the He 178, and with the experimental rocket-powered He 176. The Lippisch project was therefore transferred to Messerschmitt AG at Augsburg in January 1939.

Powered by a 660 lb thrust Walter R I-203 rocket motor, developed by Helmut Walter of Kiel, the DFS 194 was first flown by Lippisch's test pilot Heini Dittmar in 1940, when a maximum speed of 310 mph was attained. This first-generation Walter rocket achieved its combustion through the interaction of T-Stoff (80 per cent hydrogen peroxide with oxyquinoline or phosphate as a stabilising agent) and Z-Stoff (an aqueous solution of calcium permanganate). It was by no means a safe mixture; from the outset, involuntary interaction as the result of fuel leakage by these substances created extremely hazardous conditions during handling, and there were numerous catastrophic explosions.

Although the performance of the DFS 194 was unspectacular, the RLM was sufficiently interested in the concept to order the construction of two prototypes under the designation Me 163. The design of these aircraft, the Me 163V1 and Me 163V2, was generally similar to that of the DFS 194, but featured a somewhat smaller fuselage with a cockpit canopy of more rounded profile, an enlarged fin and rudder and a smaller wing with increased trailing edge sweepback.

The Me 163V1 made its first unpowered flights from Lechfeld and Augsburg in the spring of 1941, the aircraft being towed to heights between 13,120 feet and 26,240 feet by a Messerschmitt Bf 110 flown by Heini Dittmar. The Me 163V1 achieved excellent gliding angles of 1:20 in normal flight and was dived at speeds of up to 528 mph. The flying qualities were very good, with the exception of some control surface flutter, which was gradually cured by careful balance adjustments.

The Me 163 project now had the wholehearted support of *Generaloberst* Ernst Udet, the RLM's Director-General of Equipment. In the summer of 1941 the Me 163V1 was moved to Peenemünde-Karlshagen, where a 1653 lb thrust Walter HWK R.II-203 rocket motor was installed. The new motor, which still used T-Stoff and Z-Stoff propellants, had a throttle control that allowed the pilot to control the thrust in steps between 330 and 1650 lb. The engine, however, was far from perfect. One major problem was that the fuel jets tended to become clogged with particles of calcium permanganate catalyst, but if too little catalyst was supplied, the thrust fluctuated violently and produced a risk of explosion. The risk was always present; on one occasion, an entire building at Peenemünde was demolished by a blast.

Despite the setbacks, flight testing of the Me 163V1 continued. Heini Dittmar soon surpassed the existing world airspeed record with speeds of up to 568 mph, the limit being set by the two-and-a-quarter minutes of rocket motor burn time at full thrust. On 2 October 1941, Dittmar and the Me 163V1 were towed to an altitude of 11,810 feet by a Bf 110. After casting off and igniting the motor, the aircraft reached a speed of 623.8 mph, the fastest so far attained by a piloted vehicle. It would have been higher but for the effect of compressibility, which affected control of the aircraft and forced Dittmar to shut down the motor.

The RLM was so impressed by this flight, which remained shrouded in secrecy until the war's end, that development of the rocket fighter was accelerated. Orders were placed for seventy examples of an operational version, the Me 163B. These were built at Messerschmitt's Regensburg factory. The prototype for the definitive fighter version was the Me 163V3, which began unpowered flight trials early in 1942. In August, Heini Dittmar suffered serious spinal injuries in a heavy landing in this aircraft, and had to withdraw from the test programme. His place was taken by Rudolf Opitz, a pre-war test pilot who had been drafted into the *Luftwaffe*.

Meanwhile, ten Me 163A training gliders were completed by the Wolf Hirth-Werke and the trials programme continued with these and with about thirty Me 163B-0 aircraft, which were allocated V (experimental) numbers. The training programme was under the direction of Wolfgang Späte and Rudolf Opitz, the former a fighter ace with seventy-two victories. In September 1942, after many delays, the rocket motor that was to power the Me 163B became available; this was the Walter 109-509A-1, which continued to use T-Stoff but switched from Z-Stoff to C-Stoff (hydrazine hydrate, methyl alcohol and water).

The programme entered a new phase early in 1943, when some Me 163Bs were fitted with two 20 mm MG 151 cannon and, redesignated Me 163Ba-1, were assigned to an operational evaluation unit called *Erprobungskommando* 16 (EK 16) under the command of Major Wolfgang Späte. On 18 August 1943, following a massive night attack in which much of Peenemünde was obliterated by the RAF, EK 16's aircraft were evacuated to Anklam, about 20 miles to the south, the Me 163s being towed by Bf 110s. From there the unit redeployed to Bad Zwischenahn, which was to be its principal training establishment.

Meanwhile, Späte had been recruiting a nucleus of experienced pilots. One of them was *Leutnant* Mano Ziegler, who had been flying Bf 109Gs on hazardous *Wilde Sau* (Wild Boar) missions against the RAF's night bombers. Ziegler arrived at Bad Zwischenahn to begin his training, first on gliders. Ziegler described his training:

> To simulate the high approach speed of the Me 163, which came in at between 100 and 130 mph, we used a number of Habicht (Hawk) sailplanes, which had had their wing spans reduced to 19 ft 6 in. Later, the wing span of these Habicht sailplanes was further reduced to 13 ft, by which time they had been dubbed the Stummel-Habicht (Stump-Hawk). Towed aloft by a Bf 110, the Stummel-Habicht was released and dived towards the airfield at about 125 mph, side-slipping on to the ground. After several weeks we were all adept at the art of making a fast, power-off landing.

> During this flight training, we were given theoretical instruction in the Me 163. There was much to learn, particularly concerning the highly volatile fuels. Soon my head was spinning with formulae and figures, and I was more than aware of the lethal nature of T-Stoff and C-Stoff, some 4400 lb of which were to be housed in the Me 163B's tanks... The slightest fracture in a fuel pipe and both pilot and aircraft would disintegrate in the subsequent blast. One of our technical instructors gave a graphic demonstration of what could happen by pouring a thimbleful of C-Stoff into a similar quantity of T-Stoff. A searing flame shot several yards across the room – a happy augury for the future...

None of us pilots had anticipated the necessity for training which, to us, seemed more suited for engineers and analytical chemists, and, as day after day passed, our impatience grew. At last, the day before our introduction to the Me 163A arrived. For the last time we operated the rocket motors on the test rigs, and the CO ordered us to assemble for a final briefing. He made no bones about the dangers that lay ahead; he stressed the vital importance of guarding against any irregularities in take-off or touchdown; a slight swerve during take-off, premature jettisoning of the undercarriage, any negative acceleration, and we would be sent back to our relatives in matchboxes!

Landing, he pointed out, was the most dangerous phase of a flight in the rocket fighter. We had to caress the runway with our Me 163 as tenderly as a lover's kiss...

What could happen to an Me 163 pilot in an accident was illustrated in gruesome fashion a while later, when *Oberleutnant* Josef Pöhs lost his life. He was killed when, on take-off, the jettisonable trolley rebounded and struck the aircraft, cutting the T-Stoff fuel lines. The aircraft crashed and, although there was no fire, the hapless pilot, trapped in his cockpit, was literally dissolved alive when the T-Stoff tank ruptured and showered him with fuel.

Ziegler described what it was like to make a powered flight in the Me 163.

Thumbs up! With a whistling the turbine in the fuel pump started revolving: the whistle became a whine, the whine a howl. I glanced at the rev counter. All correct. I signalled to the mechanic to switch off. I freed the throttle and waited for the detonation of the blending fuels.

Bang! The first three nozzles had ignited. So far so good. The Komet was still at rest, two small blocks no more than two inches in height holding her steady until the desired thrust was attained. I glanced at the pressure indicator and threw the switch for the second stage. Two seconds later the third stage, and with a deafening roar the rocket motor opened up at full blast, the wheels jumped the tiny blocks and the machine was gathering speed down the runway. During the first two hundred yards of my take-off run I was preoccupied with the pressure indicator. The pressure in the rocket's chamber had to be 340 lb/sq in, and it was vitally necessary to ensure that it did not drop below 256 lb/sq in. In such an eventuality I had to switch off the engine immediately and just hope for the best. Simultaneously, I had to ensure that my take-off run was perfectly straight, but this was not difficult once the Komet had reached speed.

The needle of the airspeed indicator flickered to the 190 mph mark and I felt the wheels leave the runway. I threw the switch jettisoning the undercarriage and my Komet lurched forward, the acceleration forcing me back into my seat. A hurried glance at the airspeed indicator – 435 mph – and I gently pulled on the stick, flashing upwards in a near vertical climb, the earth receding at a startling speed.

The exhilaration of that first climb is indescribable. For the first time I felt at one with this remarkable aircraft. The Walter rocket thundered away behind me, but its deafening roar did not reach my consciousness, and I gave no thought to those lethal T-Stoff tanks on either side of my seat, which could turn me into a ball of fire without a second's warning. I was completely lost in the ecstasy of that seemingly endless climb. Above me stretched the wide violet canopy of the sky, and I felt completely detached from the earth below...

My Komet shuddered slightly and the rocket motor cut out. My fuel was exhausted and the drag was straining my body against the seat straps. I eased the throttle back to zero, levelled off, and reported to the control tower. I pushed the nose down slightly and now had some ten minutes of gliding flight available to examine the fighter's behaviour. I trimmed the plane carefully and then pulled the stick back slowly to discover what would happen in a stall.

Virtually nothing happened. The airflow broke away, but the plane remained horizontal, dropping gently like an elevator. I pushed the stick forward, and immediately the speed began to build up. Port wing down, and I was in a steep dive, the airflow sounding like a hurricane against my canopy... by now the altimeter indicated some 25,000 feet, and at the speed of 560 mph that I had attained, my Mach number was 0.82, not much below the Komet's limiting Mach number, so I pulled back on the stick before compressibility began to manifest itself. As the nose came up the fighter began to climb, and despite the lack of power, I had soon regained most of the altitude that I had lost in my dive...

In May 1944 Wolfgang Späte was transferred to the Eastern front to take command of IV/JG 54, a Focke-Wulf Fw 190 fighter unit, to update his operational experience. Command of EK 16 passed to *Hauptmann* Toni Thaler. At the same time, the nucleus of the first Me 163 *Jagdgeschwader*, JG 400, came into being at Wittmundhaven under the command of *Leutnant* Robert Olejnik, who had survived a serious Me 163 crash while training with EK 16. At this time, JG 400 consisted of a single *Staffel*, with only one operational Me 163; this total rose to thirteen by the end of August. During the intervening period JG 400 lost two of its aircraft to enemy action, in an air attack on Bad Zwischenahn, with five more destroyed in accidents.

In the late summer the *Staffel* was elevated to *Gruppe* status (I/JG 400). Meanwhile, EK 16 had reached initial operational capability

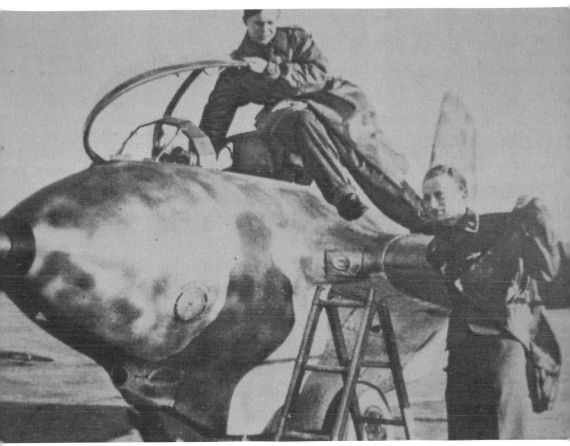

A Messerschmitt Me 163 pilot of JG 400 getting ready for a sortie. The Germans nicknamed the Me 163 Kraft Ei *(Power Egg).*

and had deployed to Brandis, where it was later joined by JG 400. The air defence task was to defend the Leuna oil refineries, which lay 56 miles to the south, from the American daylight bombers. A second *Gruppe* was formed later at Stargard, near Stettin, to defend the oil refineries at Pölitz, but this never became fully operational.

In December 1944 Wolfgang Späte returned to Germany to take command of JG 400. He was doubtless disappointed that his original plan to position flights of Me 163s on the US bombers' approach routes had not been implemented, and never would be. His intention had been to use the rocket fighters in slashing hit-and-run attacks, dislocating the bomber formations and their fighter escorts so that the conventional German fighter force might have some chance of success against much greater odds.

The Me 163's tactics were simple enough. Taking off on its jettisonable trolley, the *Komet* would climb initially at 11,811 feet per minute, this rate rising to 33,465 feet per minute at 32,000 feet. The time taken to reach the Me 163's operational ceiling of 39,698 feet was a mere 3.35 minutes; the maximum powered endurance was eight minutes. With its fuel exhausted, the Me 163 would make high-speed gliding attacks on its targets, using its two MK 108 30 mm cannon and Revi 16B gunsight. With its 120 rounds of ammunition used up and its speed starting to drop, the Me 163 would then dive steeply away from the combat area and glide back to base, landing on its retractable skid.

This in itself was a hazardous procedure, as there was always a risk of explosion if any unburnt rocket fuel remained in the aircraft's tanks. About 300 Me 163s were built, but JG 400 remained the only operational unit. The rocket fighter recorded only sixteen kills during its brief career, nine gained by JG 400 and the rest by EK 16. The Me 163C, the last version to be built for operational use, had a pressurised cockpit, an improved Walter 109–509C motor, and featured a bubble canopy on a slightly lengthened fuselage. Only a few examples were produced, and these were not issued to units. The Me 163C was to have been fitted with a novel armament arrangement developed by Dr Langwiler (inventor of the *Panzerfaust* one-man anti-tank weapon) comprising five vertically mounted tubes in each wing, each tube containing a 50 mm shell. The equipment was activated by a photo-electric cell as the rocket fighter passed under an enemy bomber. This armament was tested by *Leutnant* Hachtel of EK 16, using first a Focke-Wulf Fw 190 and then an Me 163B-1a. It was shown that it was possible for the rocket fighter to score a hit simply by flying under a bomber at full speed, the bomber's shadow activating the photo-electric cell. *Leutnant* Fritz Kelb of EK 16 tested the equipment operationally, and shot down a B-17G Fortress.

The final development of the aircraft was the Me 163D, which incorporated substantial redesign, including a retractable undercarriage. The aircraft was redesignated Me 263, a single prototype being built in 1944.

The various elements of JG 400 began to disband in February 1945, the idea being to release experienced pilots to the Messerschmitt Me 262 jet fighter units. Among them was Wolfgang Späte, who was assigned to the first *Luftwaffe* jet fighter unit,

Jagdgeschwader 7. He gained five more victories while flying the Me 262, making him one of the first jet aces. In 1956 he joined the new German *Luftwaffe*, in which he served until 1967.

Rudolf Opitz remained in command of the remaining Me 163s. In the last weeks of the war they were assembled at Husum in II/JG 400, under his command. On 22 April 1945, with the end of the war only days away, the temperamental rocket fighter nearly claimed Opitz's life, when the fire warning light came on as he was starting his take-off run in an Me 163 that had experienced problems earlier. Too late to abort the take-off, he pulled back on the stick, at the same time starting to dump the remaining fuel. With smoke filling the cockpit, he brought the Me 163 back around to try to land, but he lost sight of the field and by now flames were starting to enter the cockpit. Opitz crash-landed straight ahead, ploughing through a stone wall. The wings were torn off the Me 163 and the aircraft exploded. Crash crews found Opitz unconscious about 30 yards from the burning aircraft. He was rushed to a hospital suffering from several broken ribs, a broken collarbone and a broken arm. He survived and eventually married Hanna, the nurse who had tended him. The couple later settled in the United States, where Opitz worked on various projects at Wright Field, Ohio. He later worked for Lycoming as supervisor of Avco-Lycoming Gas Turbine Flight Test Operations, Stratford, Connecticut.

CHAPTER ELEVEN

The Parasite
Fighters

The 'parasite fighter' concept, in which a bomber or reconnaissance aircraft carries its own protective fighter, dates back to the First World War. Early in 1916, with Britain's air defences unable to cope with the threat posed by German Zeppelins, two Royal Navy officers – Commander N.F. Usborne and Lieutenant-Commander de Courcy W.P. Ireland – began to experiment with the idea of an SS-type non-rigid airship being used as a 'mother ship' for a BE.2c aircraft. The intention was that the aircraft would be carried aloft by the airship, which with its greater endurance, would be able to cruise around for several hours on the lookout for incoming Zeppelins. When one was sighted, the aircraft would be released from its position under the airship's hull to make its attack on the raider. It was an excellent idea in principle, but in practice it ended in disaster. During a trials flight on 21 February 1916, the aircraft became detached prematurely and went out of control, crashing and killing both occupants.

On 12 December 1918, the US Navy non-rigid airship C-1, commanded by G. Crompton, carried a Curtiss JN-4 biplane to a height of 25,000 feet and released it. It was the first time this experiment had been undertaken in the United States. The aircraft, piloted by A.W. Redfield, glided safely to earth. Interest in the concept, however, was not revived until a decade later, when further experiments were carried out by the US Navy's rigid airship ZR-3 *Los Angeles*, formerly the German Zeppelin LZ.126. On 27 August 1929 she picked up an aircraft in flight over Lakehurst, New Jersey, at 2500 feet and released it again from a specially designed trapeze.

In September 1931 the giant American rigid airship ZRS-4 *Akron*, one of whose features was a built-in hangar, big enough to accommodate five pursuit aircraft, had its first flight. These could be launched and taken on board again during normal cruising flight by means of a trapeze lowered through a trapdoor in the bottom of the hull. Pilots called this manoeuvre 'belly bumping'. It was a success: on one exercise, six pilots made 104 take-offs and hook-ons in the space of three hours.

During her eighteen months of US Navy service, the *Akron* took part in several fleet manoeuvres. It demonstrated the value of the airship-aircraft combination by launching air patrols over the surface forces at times when surface weather conditions made operations by carrier aircraft hazardous, if not impossible. However, the experiments ceased abruptly in April 1933, when the *Akron* broke up in severe turbulence over the Atlantic.

In the 1930s, many experiments were undertaken in the Soviet Union to find ways of adapting existing fighter designs for long-range escort duties. One of the possibilities investigated was the use of 'parasite fighters', where the fighter was carried on board the bomber and launched to provide on-the-spot defence in the target area, afterwards being retrieved in flight. The responsibility for working out the technical details was given to Vladimir S. Vakhmistrov, a member of the Scientific Research Institute of the Red Air Force, who had already designed a number of small gliders that were carried aloft by aircraft and then released for use as aerial gunnery targets.

Parasite fighter experiments began in December 1931, with two I-4 fighters attached to the upper surface of the wings of a TB-1 bomber. The two fighters were flown by test pilots Alexander Anisimov and Valerii Chkalov, with Adam Zalevski piloting the TB-1. The experiment nearly ended in disaster when the TB-1's co-pilot released the attachment of Chkalov's I-4 too soon and without warning, causing the fighter to pitch up violently. Chkalov's skill, however, saved the situation. Both fighters separated safely from the parent aircraft, carrying out a simulated mission before flying back to land at their base.

Further development of the idea was ordered by the C-in-C of the Soviet armed forces. More experiments were carried out in April 1934, this time with two I-5s attached to a four-engined TB-3 bomber, and later with two Polikarpov I-16s attached. The fact that these experiments were successful was due entirely to the exceptional skill of the test pilots; it was quickly realised that fighters would have to be specially designed for missions of this type if they were to be performed by an average Red Air Force pilot.

Vakhmistrov accordingly took a Grigorovitch TsKB-7 fighter and modified it extensively, giving it the designation I-Z (*Istrebitel Zvyeno*, literally linked fighter). The I-Z was extremely sturdy and robust, featuring stressed-skin construction. Hook-on experiments with this type began in 1934, and in April of that year test pilot Vasilii Stepanchonok successfully linked up with a special trapeze slung under a parent TB-3 bomber, afterwards detaching the I-Z and bringing it in to land safely.

Nevertheless, the use of the I-Z was seen only as an interim measure. Vakhmistrov's real hopes were pinned on a version of the Polikarpov I-17, fitted with a retractable hook, and on a projected design for a huge mother aircraft capable of carrying up to six fighters. In 1937, however, Vakhmistrov's plans received a severe blow when his chief supporter, Marshal Tukhachevski, was arrested and shot during one of Stalin's infamous purges. Vakhmistrov's funds were drastically cut, and he was forced to abandon the idea of an advanced *Zvyeno* combination. Some further experiments were made with SPB (modified I-16) fighters slung under the wings of a TB-3-AM-34 bomber. In fact, this combination was used operationally on one occasion in August 1941, when two SPBs dive-bombed a bridge in Romania after being carried within range by a TB-3.

One of the most unorthodox parasite fighters ever designed, and potentially one of the most lethal – to anyone unfortunate enough to fly it – was the McDonnell XF-85 Goblin. The project originated in 1942 as the MX-472, and revolved around the notion of a 'parasite' escort fighter that could be launched and retrieved by the bomber itself. By 1944, the USAAF requirement was more specific in that it called for a parasite fighter that could be carried by the existing Boeing B-29 and the proposed Northrop B-35 and Convair B-36 strategic bombers. McDonnell Aircraft submitted four separate proposals under the company designation Model 27 in the autumn of that year.

The problems involved in successfully launching and recovering an escort fighter were severe enough, but in January 1945 they were compounded ever further by a revised USAAF specification that required the parasite fighter to be completely housed inside the parent bomber. No designer in the world could have produced a fighter small enough to be buried inside a B-29, but the mighty B-36 was quite a different matter, and the McDonnell design team, led by project engineer Herman D. Barkey, set about revising the Model 27 to meet the new demand.

The extraordinary aircraft that gradually evolved resembled nothing so much as a large egg fitted with flying surfaces. A Westinghouse J34-WE-7 turbojet occupied almost the whole of the egg; the pilot sat astride the engine and was virtually surrounded by tanks containing 112 gallons of fuel, enough for about half an hour's flying. Also packed into the nose of the egg were four 0.5 in machine-guns. The XF-85's wings were swept 37 degrees at the leading edge, had an anhedral of four degrees and folded vertically upwards for stowage inside the parent aircraft. The tail assembly was complex, with no fewer than six surfaces. The pilot was equipped with a small ejection seat that was operated by a charge of cordite, an oxygen bottle and a ribbon-type parachute, designed to withstand heavy shock loadings at high speeds.

The XF-85 mock-up was approved in June 1946, and in March the following year McDonnell received a contract for the construction of two prototypes. At the same time, the USAAF instructed Convair to modify all B-36s from the twenty-third production aircraft to mount a trapeze for the parasite fighter in the forward bomb bay, the requirement now being for thirty operational F-85s to be purchased during 1949. Two schemes were mooted for the operational use of the F-85; one involved a single fighter to be carried by each B-36 and another suggested that an attacking force of B-36s should be accompanied by a small number of specially modified B-36s, each capable of carrying three F-85s.

In August 1947, following a change in strategic requirements, the USAF (as it now was) cancelled the order for thirty production F-85s. Work on the two XF-85 prototypes continued, however, and a bomber – the EB-29B 'Monstro' (44-8411) – was fitted with a trapeze to engage the little fighter's retractable hook. The first XF-85, 46-523, was flown in a C-47 transport to the Ames Laboratory at Moffatt Field for wind tunnel tests and suffered an immediate mishap when it was dropped from a crane. However, by June 1948 it had been repaired and taken to Muroc for flight testing, together with the second XF-85, 46-524.

On 23 August 1948, after making five captive flights, the second XF-85 was taken aloft by the EB-29 for its first free flight, with test pilot Edwin Schoch at the controls. At 20,000 feet, with the trapeze fully lowered, Schoch started the XF-85's engine and successfully unhooked himself from the parent aircraft, diving away to carry out a series of manoeuvres at speeds of between 180 and 250 mph.

Attempts at hooking up, however, presented severe problems because of turbulence, and on the fourth attempt Schoch overshot, striking the trapeze and shattering his canopy. With his helmet and oxygen mask ripped away by the airflow, he had no alternative but to dive sharply away and head for Muroc, where he touched down successfully at 160 mph on the steel skid fitted beneath the XF-85's fuselage.

Schoch spent the best part of the next two months practising approaches to the EB-29 in a Lockheed F-80 Shooting Star before taking the XF-85 into the air again on 14 October 1948. On this occasion, he successfully engaged the trapeze on his second attempt and was hoisted aboard the parent aircraft. Two more flights, made on the following day, were also successful, but then a new problem arose. Until now, the XF-85 had flown with its hook extended all the time, the well into which it was recessed on retraction being faired over. With the fairing removed, the aircraft proved to be so unstable because of turbulence around the well that a hook-up was impossible.

Flight testing was temporarily suspended while modifications were carried out; these included the fitting of vertical surfaces at

The McDonnell XF-85 Goblin was one of the most unorthdox aircraft ever built, and one of the most difficult to fly.

the wing tips to improve stability, and a metal fairing along the sides of the hook-well to smooth the airflow. On 18 March 1949, after two captive flights, Schoch and the second XF-85 were launched in free flight again, but trouble struck immediately when part of the trapeze fouled the XF-85's nose and broke away. Schoch took the XF-85 back to Muroc for yet another hair-raising skid landing on the dry lake bed. It was the last time the second XF-85 ever flew.

The first XF-85, which returned to Muroc in March 1948 after modification, was destined to make only one flight. This took place on 8 April, the aircraft flying back to Muroc after three unsuccessful attempts to hook on. Further testing of the type was suspended, at least until the trapeze had been redesigned, both the USAF and McDonnell quite rightly believing that if a pilot of Schoch's experience was unable to achieve a successful hook-up, the average fighter pilot would stand little chance of doing so. In the event, the XF-85 never flew again, although McDonnell proposed a more conventional development capable of a speed of Mach 0.9. The second XF-85 was eventually presented to the Air Force museum at Wright-Patterson AFB, while the first went to the Air Museum at Orange County Airport, Santa Ana. Between them, the two aircraft had accumulated a total flight time of 2 hours 19 minutes, the highest recorded speed being 362 mph. It would have been interesting to see whether the XF-85 would have been capable of coming anywhere near its rather optimistically estimated maximum speed of 664 mph at sea level.

In 1951, the USAF, concerned about the losses inflicted by MiG-15 jet fighters on unescorted B-29 bombers over North Korea, resurrected the parasite fighter programme under the title FICON (Fighter Conveyor). The plan now was to use a Convair B-36 to carry a Republic F-84 Thunderjet, and an RB-36F (the reconnaissance version of the huge bomber) was suitably modified and designated GRB-36F. This made its first contact flight with the fighter on 9 January 1952, which was followed, on 23 April, by the first in-flight retrieval and launch of an F-84E. On 14 May the first composite flight was made, with the Thunderjet positioned in the bomb bay during take-off and landing.

By 20 February 1953 the composite GRB-36F/F-84E had completed 170 airborne launches and retrievals, paving the way for further trials with a swept-wing F-84F Thunderstreak. The idea now was that the B-36 could be used to carry an RF-84F Thunderflash reconnaissance fighter; the latter would be launched at some point

A Republic F-84F Thunderstreak pilot makes a cautious approach and is retrieved by the Convair B-36 'mother ship'.

outside hostile territory, up to 2800 miles from the B-36's base, at an altitude of 25,000 feet. It would then fly 1180 miles to make a dash over the target at high speed (580 mph at 35,000 feet or 630 mph at sea level), after which it would be retrieved by the parent aircraft. It was a desperate idea born of desperate times.

In May 1953, contracts were awarded to Convair and Republic for the modification of ten B-36Ds into carrier aircraft and twenty-five RF-84s as parasites, the types being redesignated GRB-36D and RF-84K. The latter weighed 29,503 lb and was armed with five cameras and four 0.5 in machine-guns. The GRB-36D retained its cameras and tail armament, all other defensive weapons being deleted, and its electronic countermeasures (ECM) equipment was moved aft to make room for installation in the bomb bay of an H-shaped cradle that was lowered to launch or retrieve the RF-84K. The Thunderflash could be refuelled in the bomb bay, and the pilot was able to leave the cockpit if necessary.

In December 1954 the 91st Strategic Reconnaissance Squadron (Fighter) – SRS (F) – was activated and attached to the 407th Strategic Fighter Wing at Great Falls AFB, the pilots being trained on standard F-84F Thunderstreaks. On 24 January 1955 the 71st SRW (F) was activated at Larson AFB, Washington, with two squadrons, the 25th and 82nd SRS (F) of basic RF-84Fs. The 91st SRS joined them there with its RF-84Ks in July. Meanwhile, the modified GRB-36Ds were being delivered to the 99th SRW at Fairchild AFB, which was nearby, and operational training between the two units was underway by the end of the year. The system presented continual difficulties, however, and the partnership lasted less than a year, the 91st SRS (F) exchanging its RF-84Ks for RF-84Fs late in

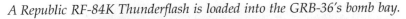

A Republic RF-84K Thunderflash is loaded into the GRB-36's bomb bay.

1956. It remained part of the 71st SRW (F) until the latter was deactivated on 1 July 1957.

In 1952–3, parasite fighter trials were also carried out in connection with Project Tom-Tom, a concept that involved two F-84F Thunderstreak fighters hooking up to an assembly fitted to a B-36's wing tips. This also started life as a fighter conveyor project, but was subsequently adapted to the strategic reconnaissance role. The aircraft used in these trials were RB-36F 49-2707 and RF-84Fs 51-1848 and 51-1849. Modifications included podded, articulated arm assemblies on the RB-36F and articulated jaw-like clamps on the RF-84Fs, to hold the parasites in position. The first hook-up was made early in 1953, using only one RF-84F, after a series of trials to determine the best approach methods. Several more hook-ups were made subsequently, but because of the enormous slipstream and wing tip vortices generated by the RB-36, the operation was extremely dangerous. The operation was terminated late in 1953 after severe oscillation caused an RF-84F to tear loose from the parent aircraft's hook-up arm.

A Republic RF-84F Thunderflash links up with a GRB-36D during a Project Tom-Tom experiment.

CHAPTER TWELVE

France's Experimentals

At the end of the war in Europe, France's aircraft industry lay in ruins, its factories destroyed or dismantled, its designers scattered far and wide. In seeking to establish a leading role in post-war aviation, therefore, France was faced with a mammoth twofold task. The first priority was an industrial one, to rebuild the factories and reassemble the design bureaux; the second was of a purely technical nature, involving the design and production of new combat types to meet the demands of the *Armée de l'Air* in the jet age.

The second priority was much harder to achieve than the first. Although some French designers had made studies of jet aircraft projects in secret during the occupation, they lagged far behind the Germans and the Allies in the field, from the viewpoint of both airframe and engine design. At the war's end, even with the knowledge that turbojet-powered aircraft were the only answer to meeting future high-performance requirements, some designers persisted in launching new piston-engined projects that resulted only in wasting time and dissipating resources.

One of the main problems that confronted the French designers was the acquisition of suitable turbojet engines. It would be a long time before turbojets of French design became available, and in the meantime two options remained open. The first was to develop an existing German turbojet, and the engine selected was the BMW 109-003, an axial-flow turbojet that stemmed from original design work carried out at Spandau by the Bramo Company in 1938. A prototype engine was tested in 1940, by which time Bramo had been taken over by BMW, and two of the first production batch were used to power the Messerschmitt Me 262V-1. Series production 109-003-A2s also powered the Heinkel He 162 and Arado Ar 234. In early post-war France, development work on the 109-003 was assigned to a team led by Dr H. Oestrich and composed of technical personnel who had worked at the Atelier Technique Aéronautique Rickenbach, a BMW plant installed near Lake Constance during the war. The factory's initials gave the new engine its name: Atar.

Production Atar 101s, however, would not be available before 1948, and so the French engineers had to exercise the second option, which was to build British turbojets under licence. In 1946, therefore, Hispano-Suiza signed a contract with Rolls-Royce for the licence production of the Nene 101 and 102 engines, and it was the latter that was to power France's first generation of jet aircraft. Yet it would be some time before the first Nenes came off the French production line, and in the meantime French designers were forced to make do with Junkers Jumo 004 turbojets to power their early experimental machines. By this time, French engineers and pilots had acquired a limited amount of jet experience with the aid of three captured Me 262s, which had been delivered to the flight test centre at Brétigny; the first one had flown on 16 June 1945, and subsequent test flying had revealed all too harshly the shortcomings of the Jumo 004 engines on which the French design bureaux, for the time being at least, were forced to rely.

It was a Jumo 004 that powered France's first experimental jet aircraft, the Sud-Ouest SO.6000 Triton, which flew for the first time on 11 November 1946 with test pilot Daniel Rastel at the controls, and also the Arsenal VG-70, which first flew on 23 June 1948. Other experimental jets were powered by Rolls-Royce Derwent engines, purchased directly from the UK; these were the SO.M-2, a flying scale model of a larger project, and the twin-jet Nord 1.601, which had originally been intended to have a pair of Rateau SRA-1s. When Rolls-Royce Nenes became available, they were earmarked to power a trio of naval fighters – the Aerocentre NC 1080, Arsenal VG-90 and Nord 2200 – as well as a twin-jet naval strike aircraft, the NC 1071. Nenes were also to have powered several land-based types: the SO.6020 Espadon fighter, the twin-jet SE.2400 attack aircraft, and the SO.4000 and NC 270 twin-jet bombers. In the event, only one early Nene-powered French design ever achieved series production; this was the Dassault MD.450 Ouragan, the first French jet fighter to be ordered in quantity.

Some of France's early jet aircraft designs were tested in scale model form, mounted on the back of a Languedoc.

Among the early Nene-powered designs was the twin-jet Sud-Ouest SO.4000 light bomber. The full-size aircraft was preceded by two scale models, the SO M-1 and M-2. The first of these, a glider, was registered F-WFDJ and was aerodynamically tested on a rig mounted on the back of a Heinkel He 274; it was subsequently mounted on Languedoc F-BCUT at Orléans-Bricy and made its first gliding flight on 26 September 1949 from a height of 16,400 feet. Before that, however, the SO M-2 (F-WFDK) had also flown on 13 April 1949, powered by a Rolls-Royce Derwent turbojet. Both scale models were piloted by Jacques Guignard, Sud-Ouest's chief test pilot, and in May 1950 he reached a speed of 621 mph while flying the M-2.

The SO.4000 bomber prototype was rolled out on 5 March 1950. Registered F-WBBL, it was generally similar in configuration to the scale models. The two crew members were seated in tandem in a small pressurised cockpit in the extreme forward fuselage, which was of large oval section. The low aspect ratio wing was swept 31 degrees at quarter-chord and was mounted in high-mid position at mid-point on the fuselage, above the weapons bay. It was planned that production aircraft should also carry an armament of two remotely controlled cannon, mounted in wing-tip barbettes. The undercarriage was complex, having four mainwheels, each with independent levered-suspension legs, and a tall single nosewheel member. The undercarriage, in fact, proved to be too fragile, because it collapsed during taxiing trials on 23 April 1950, causing extensive damage.

Repaired and with a strengthened undercarriage, F-WBBL flew for the first time on 15 March 1951, with Daniel Rastel at the controls. The aircraft proved to be seriously underpowered and unstable, and it never flew again. Sud-Ouest subsequently turned its attention to meeting a French Air Staff specification, issued in July 1951 and calling for an aircraft capable of fulfilling three separate tasks: all-weather interception, close support and medium- and high-level bombing. This was to emerge as the SO.4050 Vautour, which first flew in October 1952 powered by Atar 101B turbojets.

It was Sud-Ouest, too, who were responsible for the manufacture of France's first post-war jet fighter, the SO.6020 Espadon (Swordfish). Its designer was Lucien Servanty, and the first prototype, the SO.6020-01 (F-WFDI) flew for the first time on 12 November 1948, powered by a Rolls-Royce Nene 102 turbojet fed through a ventral air intake under the rear fuselage. This intake arrangement caused many problems, and the second prototype, the SO.6020-02 (F-WFDV), which flew on 15 September 1949, featured flush air intakes under the wing trailing edges. A third prototype, the SO.6020-03 (F-WFRG) flew on 28 December 1949 and was fitted with a long ventral air intake, a fairing at the rear of which housed a SEPR 251 liquid-fuel rocket motor; it was redesignated SO.6025 shortly afterwards. The fourth prototype, the SO.6021 (F-WFKZ), flew on 3 September 1950 and featured a lighter structure, servo controls and an increased wing area. In 1952, the SO.6020-01 first prototype was retrospectively fitted with a ventral air intake and a Turbomeca Marboré turbojet was also intalled at each wing tip, while -02 was fitted with a SEPR 251 rocket motor, fed via wing tip fuel tanks. In its new guise it was redesignated SO.6026, and on 15 December 1953 it reached Mach 1.0 in level flight over Istres. By this time, however, Dassault's Ouragan and Mystère II fighters (powered by the Atar 101) were coming off the production line, and further development of the Espadon was abandoned.

The other early Nene-powered land-based design, the Sud-Est SE.2400 attack aircraft, developed into the SE.2410 Grognard ('Grumbler', a name bestowed upon the soldiers of Napoleon's Old Guard). The prototype, the SE.2410 Grognard I, first flew on 30 April 1950, powered by two Hispano-Suiza Nene 101s mounted one above the other in the rear fuselage and with wings swept at an angle of 47 degrees. The aircraft reached a maximum speed of 645 mph at 5,000 feet. The second prototype, the SE.2415 Grognard II, flew on 14 February 1951 and was a two-seater with a sweepback of 32 degrees. This aircraft attained a maximum speed of 596 mph, but trouble was experienced with tail flutter and then the aircraft

Some of France's early jet designs, like the NC 1071 naval strike aircraft, were notable only for their ugliness.

was damaged in a belly landing as a result of a false fire warning in the air. While trials with the two prototypes progressed, albeit at a much slower rate than had been anticipated, Sud-Est's designers were working on the details of the production version, which was designated SE.2418 and which was to have been powered by two Rolls-Royce Tay turbojets. The finalised aircraft had an estimated maximum speed of 675 mph at sea level, and armament was to have comprised two 30 mm DEFA cannon and a combination of rockets and bombs. However, Sud-Ouest's promising Vautour design, was adopted to meet the *Armée de l'Air*'s ground attack requirements, and further development of the Grognard was abandoned.

Of the Nene-powered shipboard prototypes, the first to fly was Aerocentre's NC 1071 twin-jet attack aircraft, on 12 October 1948. The pilot was F. Lasne, with M. Blanchard as flight engineer. A sole prototype was produced, and development came to an end when Aerocentre went into voluntary liquidation in the summer of 1949. The company's factory at Bourges was absorbed into the Nord (SNCAN) group. This company was made responsible for the further development of another Aerocentre design, the NC.1080 single-engined naval fighter, which test pilot Lasne took into the air for the first time on 29 July 1949. The prototype, however, was totally destroyed in a flying accident on 7 April 1950.

It was Marcel Dassault who won the race to give the *Armée de l'Air* a series of interceptors that would bring France to technical parity with any other nation in the world during the 1950s. Dassault was already a very experienced designer. He was formerly Marcel Bloch, whose fighter and bomber designs had been in the *Armée de l'Air*'s front line at the outbreak of the Second World War. His refusal to co-operate with the Germans after the fall of France, together with the fact that he was Jewish, resulted in his arrest and incarceration in Buchenwald concentration camp in 1944. After the war he changed his name to Dassault, which had been his code-name in the French Resistance.

Dassault's first jet fighter, the Ouragan, was designed, built and flown in fourteen months. Thereafter, it was a relatively simple step to produce a follow-on aircraft based on the Ouragan's design, but with fully swept flying surfaces. This emerged as the Mystère I, which first flew on 23 February 1951 powered by a Nene 104B, and it was followed by two further prototypes designated Mystère IIA, powered by Tay 250 turbojets. Three pre-production machines were also Tay-powered, but the remainder were fitted with the Atar 101; this engine also powered the production aircraft, which entered

Armée de l'Air service as the Mystère IIC. Problems with the aircraft soon became apparent, however, and it experienced a series of fatal crashes caused by structural failure. It was consequently overtaken on the production line by the more advanced Mystère IVA, which had been developed in parallel with the Mystère IIC, and which proved to be a superb combat aircraft. In the mid-1950s, the fact that French combat aircraft were becoming world-beaters was underlined by the first flight, on 2 March 1955, of the Super Mystère B.1, powered by an Avon RA.7R; on the following day, it became the first aircraft of European origin to exceed Mach 1.0 in level flight at 40,000 feet.

More surprises, illustrating the advanced thinking of Dassault's design team, were on the way. In 1952, to meet a Ministry requirement for a lightweight, high-altitude, rocket-assisted interceptor capable of using grass strips, Dassault had begun the design of a small single-seat delta aircraft designated MD-550. Renamed Mirage I, it flew for the first time on 25 June 1955, powered by two Bristol Siddeley Viper turbojets. In May 1956 the Mirage I reached Mach 1.15 in a shallow dive. On 17 December 1956, with the additional boost of a SEPR 66 rocket motor, it attained Mach 1.3 in level flight.

The Mirage I, which was too small and lacked sufficient power to be an effective interceptor in its own right, was regarded by Dassault as the development aircraft for the Mirage II, which was to be powered by two Turboméca Gabizo turbojets fitted with reheat. Before the Mirage I had begun its transonic trials, however, Dassault had already decided to abandon the Mirage II in favour of a larger and more powerful variant, powered by an afterburning SNECMA Atar 101G-2 turbojet. This aircraft eventually few in prototype form on 17 November 1956, as the Mirage III-01.

The Mirage I, progenitor of one of the world's most successful lines of combat aircraft, was in direct competition with two government-backed projects, the Nord 1500 Griffon and the SO.9000 Trident.

Like Dassault, Nord Aviation based its design on a delta-wing configuration, following the pattern of an earlier high-speed research prototype, the Nord 1402 Gerfaut I. This machine, which made its first flight on 15 January 1954, was the first high-powered jet delta-wing aircraft to fly in France, and on 3 August 1954 it became the first aircraft to exceed Mach 1.0 in level flight without the use of an afterburner or rocket power. The diminutive aircraft had a wing span of only 21 feet, and was powered by a SNECMA

Atar 101D-3 turbojet. A second prototype, the Gerfaut IB, had larger wings; it exceeded the speed of sound in level flight for the first time on 11 February 1955. An uprated version, the Gerfaut II, flew on 17 April 1956 and subsequently made many supersonic test flights. The Gerfaut II's rate of climb was quite startling; it was able to reach 49,200 feet in 3 minutes 56 seconds, from a standing start.

The Nord 1500 Griffon was essentially a research aircraft too, although it had definite interceptor potential. From the outset, it was designed to test an airframe design capable of being equipped with a combination turbojet-ramjet propulsion unit. The prototype 1500-01 Griffon I made its first flight on 20 September 1955, powered only by a SNECMA Atar 101F turbojet with afterburner; after the completion of the first phase of testing, the airframe was modified to take a propulsion unit consisting of an Atar 101E engine and a Nord ramjet. Under this new guise, the aircraft was redesignated 1500-02 Griffon II. It flew for the first time on 23 January 1957, and on 17 May it exceeded Mach 1.0 in level flight with its ramjet ignited, although the full power of the combination unit was not used. As far as it is known, this was the first time that a piloted ramjet-powered aircraft exceeded the speed of sound. No combat aircraft was developed from the Griffon, which went on flying into the 1960s under a US research contract.

Sud-Ouest's design, the SO.9000 Trident, was based on the potentially lethal combination of turbojet and rocket power. Design studies began as early as 1949, and building of the first prototype, the SO.9000-01 Trident I, began at Courbevoie in October 1951. At a time when swept or delta-wing planforms were considered mandatory for supersonic flight, the Trident's designer, Lucien Servanty, took the bold step of selecting a short, thin, unswept wing spanning less than thirty feet, mounted on a bullet-like fuselage and having a Turboméca Marboré II turbojet attached to each wing-tip.

The prototype Trident I flew for the first time on 2 March 1953 at Melun-Villaroche, under the power of its wing-tip-mounted Marborés. It appeared publicly at Le Bourget in July that year, where it failed to make much of an impression alongside more exotic swept-wing types. Meanwhile, a second prototype, the SO.9000-02, was also nearing completion, and this machine made its maiden flight on 30 August 1953; it was also its last, because it crashed and was a total write-off.

Meanwhile, Sud-Ouest had been building the prototype of a more advanced version, which was to be the forerunner of a fully operational variant. Designated SO.9050 Trident II, this machine made its first flight under turbojet power only at Melun-Villaroche on 17 July 1955. The flight plan called for the Trident to take off with rocket assistance; it was then to climb to 20,000 feet, where the rocket motor was to be re-lit. The aircraft was then to make a full-power climb until its rocket fuel was exhausted.

The test pilot Charles Goujon described the flight, which was made by *Commandant* Marias. Following its initial climb, the Trident levelled off at 20,000 feet and Marias' voice came over the R/T.

Contact, chamber one.

A burst of black smoke behind the aircraft. Then the flame. The immense flame that seems to run in pursuit of the Trident and climb with it in the assault on the sky. Marias' experience now enabled him to gauge the most favourable angle of climb.

OK, Commandant? *Pierrot (in ground control) murmurs into the microphone.*

26,000, 28,000, 30,000 feet … Mach .78, .80, .82 …

Gilles looks at his chrono. Only a few seconds more before burn-out. Pierrot counts, then calls 'cut-off' on receiving word from Marias. From the ground, we can see the cloud that signals the extinction of the rocket motor. Commandant *Marias, chief test pilot of the Flight Test Centre at Brétigny, has just broken every climb record …*

A second Trident II prototype, the SO.9050-002, was destroyed on its first flight that same month, but Charles Goujon went on to fly -001 to a speed of Mach 1.7 (1122 mph), at that time the highest speed attained by any piloted aircraft in Europe. In January 1956 an order for six pre-production machines was placed by the French Air Ministry, and the first of these flew on 3 May 1957.

Then came tragedy. On 21 May 1957, Trident-001 was destroyed during a test flight when its highly volatile rocket fuels, furaline and nitric acid, became accidentally mixed and caused an explosion. The pilot, Charles Goujon, was killed. Further development of the Trident was halted shortly afterwards.

In seeking to develop their new generation of combat aircraft French designers took conscious risks; five French test pilots were killed in 1957 alone, and others injured, one of them while testing the most curious aircraft of all, the Leduc 010 ramjet.

René Leduc's experiments with ramjet-powered aircraft dated back to 1937. A small research ramjet designated Leduc 010 eventually took to the air in November 1946, mounted on the back of a Bloch 161 transport, making its first gliding flight on 21 October 1947. On 21 April 1949, after a series of gliding trials, it took to the air for the first time with ramjet lit, and on 31 May that year it reached a speed of 905 km/h (562 mph) at 7625 m (25,000 ft). Subsequent testing was not trouble-free; on 27 November 1951 it was badly damaged in a crash-landing, its pilot being seriously injured, and on 25 July 1952, after repair, it struck its Languedoc launch aircraft on release and had to make a belly landing.

Meanwhile, Leduc had been building a larger and more powerful ramjet research vehicle, the Leduc 021. Air tests began on 16 May 1953, with the aircraft mounted above a Languedoc, and several gliding trials were made before the first powered flight on 7 August 1953. Subsequent flight trials were carried out throughout the flight envelope up to a limiting Mach number of 0.85. Among other spectacular performance figures the 021 showed an initial climb rate of 200 m/sec (39,370 ft/min) and a ceiling of 20,000 m (65,600 ft). A second Leduc 021 was built, and this flew under its own power for the first time on 1 March 1954. The 021's pilot was accommodated semi-reclined in a bullet-like nose fairing that protruded from the main engine tube; it could be jettisoned in an emergency, a parachute system being located immediately aft of the pilot. Aft of the cabin, the central body contained the Turboméca Artouste I turbine, which drove the fuel pumps and generators, together with fuel tanks, batteries and radio. Aft of this central core were twenty-one burners, arranged in seven banks through which fuel was sprayed; each bank could be lit separately, depending on the amount of power required.

The Leduc 021 was designed to be the research vehicle for an operational interceptor, and as the next step towards this goal a more advanced prototype, the Leduc 022, was designed and built. The 022 was larger than its predecessors and had swept flying

The extraordinary Leduc 021 was intended to be the test vehicle for a fully-fledged ramjet interceptor.

surfaces; it was equipped with an Atar 101D-3 turbojet, installed inside the ramjet duct, that enabled the aircraft to take off under its own power and accelerate to the point where the ramjet could take over. The aircraft flew for the first time on 26 December 1956 and quickly showed enormous performance potential, including an ability to climb to 25,010 m (82,000 ft) in four minutes. With flight testing of of 022-01 well underway, construction of a second prototype was started. However, the 022's limiting factor was endurance; at an estimated maximum combat speed of Mach 2.4 (it actually achieved Mach 1.5 during its trials) the aircraft could carry sufficient fuel for only ten minutes' flying.

Besides, French Air Ministry requirements were now turning more towards the concept of multi-role combat aircraft, a policy dictated by wildly escalating research and development costs. The day of the pure interceptor was over, and the Leduc 022, one of the most radical aircraft designed anywhere during the post-war years of experiment, was abandoned.

CHAPTER THIRTEEN

Combat Flying Boats: the Jet Age's Lost Cause

Although the Second World War witnessed great strides in the development of flying boats for the long-range maritime reconnaissance role, little attention was paid to the use of seaplanes to fill other combat requirements until the closing months of the Pacific war, when the British Air and Naval Staffs issued a joint specification, E6/44, for a single-seat twin-jet water-based fighter.

In 1944, preparations were underway to send a Royal Navy task force formed around a nucleus of five fleet carriers to the Pacific Theatre to support the United States' effort there. This was to be followed, late in 1945, by Tiger Force, comprising several squadrons of Lancasters, Lincolns and Mosquitoes of the RAF. At this stage, no one knew how long the Pacific war might drag on; the atomic bomb was still in the future as an operational weapon.

Because of the vast distances involved, the aircraft carrier – and, eventually, the long-range B-29 bombers of the USAAF – remained the only means of carrying the war to the Japanese homeland. Aircraft carriers, however, were vulnerable to air attack, as were the bases on the newly-captured islands that would be used as springboards for the final assault on Japan. The extent to which Japan's offensive capability was becoming depleted was not yet known, and the British, with bitter memories of campaigns lost in the early days of the war because air bases were knocked out by enemy air attack, were determined to take out some kind of insurance against the possibility of it happening again. The result was E6/44.

After some preliminary studies, a team led by Henry Knowler of Saunders-Roe Ltd submitted a design for a jet fighter flying boat intended for operation from sheltered coastal waters such as the bays and lagoons that were a feature of many Pacific islands. With no advanced flying boat design data to draw upon, Knowler and his team decided to go for a conventional hull, with a length-to-beam ratio of approximately 6:1, even though this would result in an aircraft with a maximum level speed considerably lower than that of a land-based counterpart. Fortunately, the nature of the specification, which did not envisage operation in open waters, made it unnecessary to raise the engine air intake to a height where there would be no possibility of flooding in rough seas, so the designers were able to keep the hull depth to a minimum.

The aircraft's twin turbojets were mounted side by side in the hull, sharing a common nose intake but exhausting through individual jet pipes. These were angled outwards at 5 degrees to keep the efflux clear of the rear fuselage. The wing was conventional, employing a high-speed section and shoulder-mounted, its leading edge just below the cockpit. The stabilising floats retracted inwards, rotating through 90 degrees in the process to form an aerodynamically clean bulge under the wing when fully retracted. The cockpit was fully pressurised. The pilot was seated under a sliding canopy and had a Martin-Baker ejection seat.

Three prototypes were ordered under the designation SRA1, and it was decided to continue building them for evaluation even after the end of the Pacific war. The first prototype, TG263, flew for the first time at East Cowes on the Isle of Wight on 16 July 1947, powered by two Metropolitan-Vickers (Metrovick) F.2/4 Beryl axial-flow turbojets. The test pilot was Geoffrey Tyson. The aircraft design was already close to meeting the operational requirement, provision being made for four 20 mm cannon above the air intake, and there were points for two flush-fitting auxiliary fuel tanks under the inboard wing sections.

The first four test flights revealed very few snags, and Saunders-Roe felt confident enough to demonstrate the SRA1 before representatives of the RAF, Royal Navy and the Royal Aircraft Establishment late in July; the aircraft was also shown to the public at the Society of British Aircraft Constructors (SBAC) air display at Farnborough in September. The other two prototypes, TG267 and

The Saunders-Roe SRA1 was aerodynamically sound and flew well, but its performance did not match that of land-based fighters.

TG271, joined the test programme in 1948; the former was fitted with an acorn-type fairing at the junction of the fin and tailplane and had a strengthened cockpit canopy. It was powered by uprated Metrovick Beryl MVB2 engines of 3500 lb thrust; the third aircraft had the fully operational version of the turbojet, the Beryl Mk 1.

The second and third SRA1 prototypes were both involved in accidents, causing serious delays to the test programme, but testing was resumed with the first prototype in 1951. By this time it was clear that the SRA1, although a surprisingly manoeuvrable aircraft, was inferior on every other count to contemporary land-based fighters, and that it had little development potential. The last remaining example of the world's first jet-powered fighter flying boat therefore went to the College of Aeronautics at Cranfield. It was subsequently acquired by the Skyfame Museum at Staverton, Gloucestershire, and then by the Southampton Hall of Aviation, where it may be seen today.

Although it did not fall into the 'dangerous aircraft' category, the SRA1 has been described at some length here to illustrate the fact that it was precisely the cautious approach of its designer that made it aerodynamically sound. This no-risk policy was far removed from the approach of US manufacturers, who sought to achieve a quantum leap in the design of a water-based jet fighter.

In the United States, there had been a drift away from flying boat development by 1944, with long-range maritime patrol tasks being increasingly undertaken by land-based aircraft such as the Liberator and Privateer. In the immediate post-war years, however, research into new hydrodynamic shapes, coupled with jet propulsion, led to a reawakening of interest in the belief that many of the earlier seaplane limitations could now be overcome. The lion's share of the research was undertaken by the US Navy Bureau of Aeronautics (BuAer), the National Advisory Committee for Aeronautics (NACA, the forerunner of NASA) and the Consolidated Vultee Aircraft Corporation (Convair). It was Convair who received a Bureau of Aeronautics contract to develop a flying boat configuration that would result in a waterborne fighter with a performance comparable with that of land-based aircraft.

The Convair design team, led by Ernest Stout, set about proving their theories in practical fashion by devising a series of scale models. The climax was the top-secret Project Skate, which involved some of the most advanced aerodynamic designs to be tested in the late 1940s. The later models employed 'blended hulls', the theory being that the aircraft rode so low in the water that their wings aided buoyancy. In these models, the wing and hull were blended in unprecedented aerodynamic cleanness; spray dams were fitted on either side of the fuselage nose to speed up take-off by deflecting the spray downwards, keeping it clear of the air intakes. Some models taxied, took off, flew and landed under radio control; others were catapult-launched, and yet others were towed behind high-speed motor launches to test spray and aerodynamic characteristics. At the same time, the NACA carried out extensive tests to find an acceptable form of undercarriage that would remove the need for conventional floats and improve hydrodynamic characteristics.

The configuration that seemed most acceptable was the hydro-ski. In this arrangement, twin hydro-skis, fitted flush against the under surface of the hull, extended like flat seaplane floats under the water. As the aircraft gathered speed, the action of the skis pushed up its fuselage until it was clear of the surface, the machine skimming the waves until take-off speed was reached. When safe flying speed was attained, the skis were retracted, leaving the aircraft aerodynamically clean.

By early 1984, the Convair blended hull concept and the NACA hydro-skis had reached an advanced stage of development, and this led to a BuAer requirement for a full-scale fighter prototype. The requirement called for an aircraft with a maximum speed of Mach 0.95 and an ability to operate in a five-foot swell. A design contest was initiated on 1 October 1948 and two designs were submitted, one by the NACA and the other by Convair; the former embodied hydro-skis and the latter the blended hull principle. The Convair design, which offered a better rate of climb and high-altitude performance, was accepted. However, the project went ahead on a relatively low budget; the US Navy's emphasis was on the development of carrier-borne jet fighters.

At this stage, further development concentrated on comparative tests between the hydro-ski and blended hull concepts. By 1950, hydro-ski development had undergone considerable advances. As a result, the US Navy's requirement changed; what was now wanted was a faster aircraft fitted with skis, and smaller in overall dimensions than the original Convair proposal. This had envisaged a large twin-engined fighter with swept flying surfaces, based on the later series of Project Skate models; to meet the new requirement, Convair now evolved a smaller delta-wing design, the Y2-2, equipped with twin hydro-skis.

The new design was aerodynamically similar to the Convair F-102 delta-wing interceptor, then being developed for the USAF. The estimated performance figures included a maximum speed of Mach 1.5 and an initial rate of climb of 30,000 feet per minute. The power was to be provided by two Westinghouse XJ46-WE-2 turbojets rated at 4080 lb thrust. However, by the time Convair received a letter of intent on 19 January 1951, it had been decided to install 3400 lb thrust Westinghouse J34-WE-32 engines in the prototype, the XJ46 development programme having been subjected to some delays.

In August 1951, the Y2-2 was redesignated XF2Y-1, and on 28 August 1952, with work on a prototype well advanced, Convair received a BuAer contract for twelve pre-series F2Y-1s.

In January 1953, the completed prototype XF2Y-1, now known as the Sea Dart, began taxiing trials in San Diego Bay, and it was during these that unexpected problems were encountered with the hydro-skis. The skis worked adequately at up to 60 mph, but beyond that they were susceptible to a phenomenon known as ski-pounding, with severe vibration that threatened to damage the airframe. Some modifications were made to the shape of the skis and to the shock absorbers between the skis and the hull, and the Sea Dart eventually made its first true flight on 9 April 1953, the aircraft already having made a 300-yard hop during a taxi run on 14 January.

The Convair XF2Y-1 Sea Dart carrying out a high-speed taxi run in San Diego Bay. Ski buffeting was a constant problem.

Meanwhile, problems had been experienced with the proposed XJ46 powerplant, which, during test runs, had failed to develop the anticipated thrust. This fact, together with some aerodynamic deficiencies that had been belatedly revealed, meant that the Sea Dart would be unlikely to exceed Mach 1. It was therefore proposed to adopt a single Wright J67 or Pratt & Whitney J75 turbojet, but then the designers realised that this would lead to an unacceptable amount of fuselage redesign and the idea was dropped.

By the autumn of 1953, with the hydro-skis still causing problems, the future for the Sea Dart looked anything but rosy. Development of one of the XF2Y-1 prototypes was abandoned in October, and in November the order for ten of the pre-series F2Y-1s was cancelled. The order for the other two pre-series aircraft was cancelled in March 1954, leaving Convair with an order for four YF2Y-1s for evaluation by the US Navy.

During 1954, more than a hundred hydro-ski modifications were tested, using both single- and twin-ski configurations, and it was found that the single-ski arrangement was more satisfactory. Ski-pounding was reduced, although stability on take-off left much to be desired and there was a tendency to porpoise.

On 3 August 1954, Convair test pilot Charles E. Richbourg took the second Sea Dart through Mach 1 in a shallow dive. This made the Sea Dart the first (and to date the only) seaplane to go supersonic. Since the Sea Dart had been designed before the advent of the area rule, the aircraft experienced high transonic drag and was unable to exceed the speed of sound in level flight. Flight tests indicated some wing spanwise airflow, and a single airflow fence was mounted on each upper wing surface near the tip. No other Sea Dart was fitted with wing fences.

The US Navy evaluation programme began on 1 November 1954, and was attended almost immediately by disaster. On 4 November, the first of the three YF2Y-1s to be built broke up during a public demonstration over San Diego Bay when Richbourg inadvertently exceeded the airframe limitations. Richbourg was fatally injured, and the evaluation programme was postponed until May 1955. Testing continued with the two remaining YF2Y-1s and the XF2Y-1 prototype, but ski difficulties persisted and the Sea Dart programme was abandoned in 1956.

In parallel with the development of the Sea Dart, the US Navy had also shown considerable interest in the potential of a jet-powered bomber/reconnaissance flying boat, and in October 1952 the Martin Aircraft Company was awarded a contract for the development of such an aircraft, the Model 275 (XP6M-1) SeaMaster. The development programme called for the construction of two XP6M-1 prototypes and six YP6M-1 evaluation aircraft, all of which were to be powered by four Allison J71-A-4 turbojets. They were to be followed by an initial production batch of twenty-four P6M-2s, powered by 15,000 lb thrust Pratt & Whitney J75-P-2 engines.

The XP6M-1 prototype first flew on 14 July 1955 and completed 79 hours of taxiing and flight testing before it crashed on 7 December 1955, following a control malfunction. The second SeaMaster flew on 18 May 1956, but that also crashed on 9 November 1956, following a failure in the hydraulic system. The first YP6M-1 evaluation aircraft, with modifications to prevent a recurrence of the disasters that had overtaken the two prototypes, flew on 20 January 1958, and this was followed by the first production P6M-2 on 17 February 1959. In all, as well as the two prototypes, six YP6M-1s and four P6M-2s were completed, but by the spring of 1959 the US Navy's research and development budget was being allocated to other programmes that were thought to be more important. Testing of the SeaMaster had revealed numerous

A very advanced concept, the Martin SeaMaster was bedevilled by accidents and malfunctions during its test phase.

technical problems – water seepage through the rotary weapons bay door in the hull was one, although this was later solved – and the cost of the programme had risen to three times the original estimate.

By this time, the number of P6M-2 SeaMasters on order had been reduced to eight, which were to have formed a single US Navy squadron. Only three P6M-2s, however, were taken on charge, and these were eventually broken up for scrap at the Patuxent River Naval Air Test Center, Maryland.

Basically, the SeaMaster's biggest drawback had been its advanced concept. It was potentially a very versatile aircraft with a high performance; the maximum speed, for example, was 654 mph (Mach 0.92) at 21,000 feet, and the unrefuelled range was 1500 miles with a 30,000 lb payload. With its ability to carry mines, bombs, torpedoes or a camera pack, the SeaMaster would have been capable of performing many roles. However, it would have needed considerable logistical support and most of the tasks it was designed to carry out could be done equally as well by a new generation of advanced carrier-borne aircraft. The demise of the SeaMaster was the final nail in the coffin of combat flying boat development in the United States.

The Russians, too, did not enjoy much success with jet-powered flying boats. At the end of the Second World War, all flying boat and seaplane research and development work in the USSR was concentrated in Georgii M. Beriev's design bureau. Priority was given to the design of a modern maritime patrol aircraft with a long endurance. The design evolved by the Beriev team was the LL-143, the 'LL' standing for *Letayushchaya Lodka*, or flying boat. It was a large, gull-winged monoplane powered by two 2000 hp Shvetsov ASh-72 radial engines, and was armed with a 23 mm cannon in the bow and paired 23 mm cannon in dorsal and tail turrets. In its definitive version, the LL-143 was ordered into production as the Be-6 (NATO reporting name: 'Madge').

Meanwhile, Beriev had been working on an advanced jet-powered flying boat, the Be-R-1. It was a good design from both the aerodynamic and hydrodynamic points of view, with a length-to-beam ratio of 8:1 and a long, narrow planing bottom that greatly reduced drag, both in the air and on the water. Moreover, the Be-R-1 was designed for operation in rough seas. The aircraft was powered by two Klimov VK-1 turbojets positioned above the shoulder-mounted gull wing, their long nacelles projecting a considerable distance forward of the leading edge. The wing and tail surfaces wre conventional and unswept. Everything in the Be-R-1's design reflected Beriev's desire to keep aerodynamic drag to a minimum; the pilot was seated under a fighter-type blister canopy, offset to port, the stabilising floats were retracted in flight to lie flush with the wing tips, and the defensive armament comprised two 23 mm cannon in a streamlined tail barbette.

The Be-R-1 underwent flight trials at Taganrog from 1949 to 1951. Although its performance was promising, including a maximum speed at sea level of 478 mph, the aircraft was not accepted for service, and it was the turboprop-powered Be-12 *Tchaika* (NATO reporting name: 'Mail') that succeeded the Be-6 in service with the Soviet Naval Air Arm.

Nevertheless, the Be-R-1 provided the Beriev team with invaluable experience in high-speed flying boat design, and in 1961 a twin-jet flying boat was publicly revealed for the first time at the Tushino air display. This was the Be-10, known to NATO as 'Mallow', which subsequently established a number of FAI-approved (Fédération Aéronautique International) records for seaplanes. A small number of Be-10s entered service with a Soviet Navy trials unit, but the type's career was brief.

Twenty years later, Beriev resurrected the maritime patrol flying boat concept in the A-40 Albatross, the world's largest amphibious aircraft, which was designed to replace the Be-12 and Ilyushin Il-38 in the maritime patrol and ASW (anti-submarine warfare) roles. Design work on the Albatross began in 1983, but it was not until 1988 that the type was made publicly known in the west, when the United States announced it had taken satellite photographs of a jet powered amphibian under development in Russia. The Albatross made its first flight in December 1986, while its first public appearance was a fly-by at the 1989 Soviet Aviation Day Display at Tushino, Moscow. In the years that followed, the A-40 established no fewer than 148 world records for aircraft of its class, yet in 2004 its production status was still uncertain. Like the Americans before them, the Russians may at last have learned that the jet-powered flying boat is not the ideal vehicle for the maritime task.

CHAPTER FOURTEEN

Russia's Early Jets: the Ugly Ducklings

Following the acquisition of the first captured German turbojets at the end of 1944, various Soviet design bureaux were ordered to begin a crash programme aimed at producing operational fighters designed around these engines. The bureaux involved were Mikoyan and Guryevich (MiG), Lavochkin, Sukhoi and Yakovlev. By the time initial design studies were nearing completion, copies of the German engines were already in production, the BMW 003 as the RD-20 and the Jumo 004 as the RD-10.

Each design bureau tackled the problem in its individual fashion, all from a starting point in February 1945. While Mikoyan and Guryevich set about designing a fighter around a pair of BMW 003A engines, Sukhoi adopted a design with twin underslung engines reminiscent of the Messerschmitt Me 262; Lavochkin came up with an aircraft built around a Jumo 004 engine mounted in a fuselage pod; while Yakovlev opted for an adaptation of their existing and well-proven Yak-3 fighter. The resulting aircraft, designated Yak-15, flew for the first time on 24 April 1946. Deliveries to Soviet Air Force fighter squadrons began early in 1947. Production aircraft retained a tailwheel undercarriage and were powered by the RD-10 engine. About 280 were built. At the time of its introduction the Yak-15 was the lightest jet fighter in the world, the lightweight structure of the Yak-3's airframe compensating for the relatively low power of the engine. The Yak-15's NATO reporting name was 'Feather'.

The MiG design was the I-300, the I standing for *Istrebitel*, or interceptor. Although the aircraft was powered by two engines, mounted side-by-side in the centre fuselage, it was by no means heavy, the loaded weight being in the region of 11,000 lb. The I-300 featured the first tricycle undercarriage installed on a Russian-built aircraft, the narrow-track mainwheels retracting outwards into the wings. Three I-300 prototypes were built, the first of which had its maiden flight on 24 April 1946 with test pilot Alexander Grinchik at the controls. During subsequent testing, the maximum speed was gradually pushed up to 566mph. Severe vibration was experienced in the higher speed range, and it took a considerable time before the cause was established. The jet efflux, exhausting under the tail, was buffeting the fireproof sheathing of the rear fuselage undersurface and setting up resonance throughout the airframe.

A month after the aircraft's first flight, while Grinchik was carrying out a high-speed, low-level run in the first prototype the aircraft suddenly developed an uncontrollable pitch and dived into the ground, killing its pilot. Grinchik's place was taken by Mark Gallai who, together with Georgii Shianov, continued the flight test programme with the two other aircraft. Gallai enjoyed enormous prestige with the elite Soviet test pilot fraternity. He came from a Jewish family, which might have been a problem for career advancement under the Soviet system, but his manifest skills as a pilot and engaging personality won him respect everywhere. His flight log included some of the most important aircraft of the period after the Second World War. Gallai flew more than 200 types of aircraft, even taking the controls of the *Luftwaffe*'s dangerous Me 163 interceptor.

Both pilots experienced a high workload, as the I-300 was difficult and often unpleasant to fly, many of its problems resulting from the haste with which it had been completed. On one occasion, Gallai almost came to grief when, during a high-speed run at Mach 0.8, the nose of the aircraft pitched down violently. He reduced power and managed to restore full control, but after landing it was found that both the tailplane and elevator had become distorted. In all probability, Gallai had experienced the problem that had killed Grinchik.

On another occasion, Gallai was carrying out a high-speed run at 2000 feet when the I-300 virtually went out of control; fortunately, the nose went up instead of down and the aircraft gained several thousand feet of altitude, vibrating badly, with the pilot practically helpless. Gallai reduced power and restored partial control, looking back to check the tail; to his dismay he saw the port tailplane was no longer there, and the starboard tailplane was badly distorted. To make matters worse, fuel from a ruptured tank was seeping into the cockpit and there was a severe fire risk. Gallai would have been quite justified in baling out, but he was a test pilot of the highest calibre. Cutting both engines, he managed to bring the aircraft back for a dead-stick landing.

Despite its vicissitudes, the I-300 was ordered into production for the Soviet Air Force as the MiG-9 and, with a redesigned nose to accommodate one 37 mm and two 23 mm cannon, was the first Russian jet type to reach squadron service, the first deliveries being made in December 1946. Although technically far from reliable, it provided Russian fighter pilots with valuable experience in jet operation.

While striving to bring the MiG-9 to production standard, Mikoyan was also studying other fighter projects. In 1946, the MiG bureau built and tested a rocket-powered target defence interceptor, the I-270 (Zh), which was based on the wartime Messerschmitt Me 263A rocket fighter project.

The first Russian attempt to produce a short-range, rocket-propelled target defence interceptor, designed to have a rate of climb of 35,400 ft/min, had been made some years earlier. This was the Bereznyak-Isayev BI-1. It was to be powered by a Dushkin D-1 rocket motor, which was successfully tested in a glider that had been towed to altitude. Of mixed construction, the BI-1, a small low-wing monoplane, was built in only forty days, and was flown as a glider for the first time on 10 September 1941. The first powered test flight was made on 15 May 1942 and was successful, but shortly afterwards the prototype was destroyed when it crashed during a maximum-power run at low level. Despite this setback seven pre-series aircraft were built and the programme went ahead. However, subsequent flight trials revealed unforeseen aerodynamic problems. Also, Dushkin's work on a multi-chamber rocket motor encountered innumerable snags, and the powered endurance of eight minutes was considered insufficient for operational purposes. All these problems brought an end to the project.

Whereas the Me 263A had been a swept-wing design, the I-270 employed an unswept wing of thin section and slightly swept horizontal tail surfaces, mounted T-fashion on top of the vertical surfaces. The Russian aircraft was powered by an RD-2M-3V bi-fuel rocket motor, which was a slightly modified version of the Walter HWK 509C; it was equipped with main and cruising chambers, the former giving a maximum endurance of 4 minutes 15 seconds and the latter 9 minutes 3 seconds. The first airframe, Zh-1, began glider tests in December 1946, towed by a Tupolev Tu-2 to its release point.

The Zh-2, rocket-powered with a dual thrust engine (1650 kg boost / 400 kg cruise), first flew in March 1947. However, the total burn time of the rocket engines was only 255 seconds, and by this time the prototype of the faster and much longer-ranged turbojet-powered MiG-15 was nearing completion. Therefore, the I-270 was seen as having no military utility and abandoned after the Zh-2 was written off in a hard landing in the spring of 1947. Under test, the I-270 reached an altitude of 32,810 feet in 2.37 minutes, and 49,215 feet in 3.03 minutes. The maximum speed was 620 mph, and the proposed armament was two 23mm cannon.

In the late 1940s Yakovlev built the prototypes of three single-seat fighter designs, none of which came to fruition. The first, in 1947, was the Yak-19, a simple and uncomplicated aircraft with unswept flying surfaces and powered by an RD-500 (based on the Rolls-Royce Derwent) turbojet. The Yak-19, in fact, served as the prototype of a more refined design, the Yak-25; this had a similar powerplant, but was fitted with swept tail surfaces and wing-tip drop tanks. The Yak-25 was intended to fulfil the same tactical role as the Republic F-84 Thunderjet, but it had extremely disappointing performance figures and was consequently abandoned. Its designation was allocated to a later – and vastly more successful – fighter type, the Yak-25 'Flashlight'.

The Yakovlev Yak-30 was built to the same specification as the MiG-15, but during comparative trials the Mikoyan fighter emerged as the better design all round.

The other Yakovlev jet fighter design of the 1940s was the Yak-30, a swept-wing fighter built to the same specification as the MiG-15. Powered by an RD-45 (Rolls-Royce Nene) turbojet, the Yak 30 first flew in 1948; the maximum speed was 640 mph, the service ceiling was 49,500 feet and the range was 900 miles. The Yak-30 underwent comparative trials with the MiG-15, from which the Mikoyan fighter emerged as the better aircraft on all counts.

In the original race to produce a jet fighter in 1945–6, Mikoyan had been ordered to design an aircraft around two Junkers Jumo 004A turbojets; the result, as we have seen, was the MiG-9, the first jet fighter to enter Russian service. Another designer with the same brief was Pavel Sukhoi, whose Su-2 ground attack aircraft had filled a dangerous gap during the war until the deployment of the Ilyushin Il-2. However, his subsequent designs, although often advanced and sometimes aerodynamically better than some that achieved production status, had laboured under a series of misfortunes – often caused by the lack of suitable engines. Consequently, they had never met with the success they deserved. Nevertheless, Sukhoi was one of Russia's most experienced aeronautical engineers, and it was logical that his expertise should be put to good use in the jet fighter development programme.

Sukhoi approached the design of his first jet fighter, the Su-9, with a good deal of caution, preferring to adopt a similar configuration to that of the Messerschmitt Me 262 – although the aircraft that emerged was by no means a copy of the German fighter. The Su-9's engines were placed in underwing nacelles and the aircraft had an Me 262-style cockpit, but there the resemblance ended. The flying surfaces were less angular and the wings were unswept, while the fuselage was deeper and slimmer than the Me 262's. The only aspect, apart from the engines, that might be said to have been copied from the Me 262 was the tricycle undercarriage. Even here, there were distinct differences.

Like the MiG-9, the Su-9 was armed with one 37 mm and two 23 mm cannon, and for short take-off a pair of solid-fuel rockets could be attached under the fuselage. The Su-9 was generally a more refined design than the MiG aircraft; among other items, it featured a compressed-air ejection seat, modelled on German equipment, and a braking parachute. The aircraft flew for the first time in 1946, some months after the MiG-9, and the performance figures for the two aircraft were not dissimilar. Although the Su-9 was slightly inferior to the MiG-9 at high altitude, its range performance adequately compensated for this, and it also carried more

The Sukhoi Su-9 had the same configuration as the Messerschmitt Me 262, but was by no means a copy of the German fighter.

ammunition. In view of the MiG-9's appalling safety record, there seemed no reason why the Sukhoi aircraft should not have been selected in preference.

But there was a reason, and it was an extraordinary one. It appears that other Soviet designers, eager to have their own aircraft accepted, 'ganged up' on Sukhoi at a conference in 1946. They persuaded Josef Stalin that any machine that resembled the Messerschmitt Me 262 would be unacceptable because the German fighter had proved dangerous to fly. Stalin was by no means an aviation expert, but he had seen photographs of the Me 262, and to his mind the Su-9 was sufficiently like it to be seen in an unfavourable light. In all probability, Stalin's concern was not so much to do with safety concerns, but more to do with a desire to show the world that the Soviet regime was capable of producing modern aircraft without being accused of copying those of its former enemy. So, after one brief appearance at the Tushino air display on 3 August 1947, the Su-9 was abandoned and the Soviet Air Force took delivery of the heavy, unwieldy MiG-9, which killed its pilots in considerable numbers.

Following this disappointment, Sukhoi now pinned his hopes on the development of two advanced jet fighter projects, the Su-15 and Su-17. By 1948, the Russians – again relying heavily on German technology – had developed an AI (airborne intercept) radar known as Izumrud (Emerald), which was intended to equip a new generation of all-weather fighter aircraft. Sukhoi's response to the specification was the Su-15, which was also known as the Samolyot P. Powered by two RD-45 turbojets, the aircraft had a mid-mounted wing with a leading edge sweep of 37 degrees. The twin engines were mounted one above the other in a deep centre fuselage and exhausted below the fuselage aft of the trailing edge. The AI scanner was housed in a small radome situated above the nose air intake, and the armament comprised two 37 mm cannon mounted one on either side of the nose. With a loaded weight of 23,000 lb, the Su-15 was a very heavy aircraft; nevertheless, its designers estimated that it would have a maximum speed of 641 mph, a service ceiling of 45,930 feet, and the ability to reach 32,800 feet in six and a half minutes. These figures were never proved, because the Su-15 disintegrated following severe vibration on an early high-speed run (the pilot ejecting), and no further prototypes were built.

Work continued in 1949 on the Su-17 supersonic fighter project, which was to have been powered by a Mikulin TR-3 axial-flow turbojet and had wings swept at 50 degrees. The estimated performance figures included speeds of Mach 1.08 at 36,090 feet and Mach 1.02 at sea level, with a service ceiling of 50,850 feet. A novel feature of the Su-17 was that in an emergency the fuselage nose, including the cockpit, was intended to be blasted clear of the rest of the airframe by explosive charges and stabilised by a drogue. The pilot would subsequently eject in normal fashion. By this time, however, Sukhoi had fallen out of favour with the Ministry for Aeronautical Development and Production. In 1949, on orders from Moscow, his factory was closed down. All work on the Su-17, the airframe of which was partially complete, was brought to a halt and the aircraft broken up for scrap. Despite these misfortunes, Pavel Sukhoi was later to bounce back into the limelight of Soviet fighter design.

The first venture into the jet fighter field by the other leading Soviet designer, Semyon A. Lavochkin, was the La-150, which was powered by a single RD-10 (Jumo 004A) turbojet. The aircraft, which was flown for the first time in September 1946 by test pilot A.A. Popov, featured a 'pod and boom' design, with unswept shoulder-mounted wings and a tricycle undercarriage mounted in the lower fuselage. The armament comprised two 23 mm NS cannon, one on either side of the nose. Two prototypes were built, and these reached a maximum speed of 500 mph at 16,400 feet; the service ceiling was 41,000 feet. Three more aircraft were completed and fitted with uprated RD-10F engines, being redesignated La-150M. However, the flight characteristics of the Lavochkin design left much to be desired – severe oscillation of the tail boom was only one of its problems – and further development was abandoned in April 1947.

Meanwhile, Lavochkin had also begun work on three more fighter prototypes, the La-152, La-154 and La-156, all of which featured a configuration that was closer in style to that of Yakovlev's Yak-15. The fuselage undercarriage arrangement was retained, but the wing was mounted at mid-point and the cockpit was positioned well aft, over the trailing edge. However, although the handling characteristics of these three aircraft were somewhat better than those of the La-150, performance was actually poorer, and they were used only for experimental flying.

By the middle of 1947, Russian designers were overcoming an early aversion to the use of sweepback (an aversion that was shared by their British and French counterparts), and Lavochkin decided to fit the basic La-152 fuselage with swept flying surfaces. The result was the La-160, which had a wing swept at the optimum 35 degrees and an armament of two NS-37 cannon. The aircraft flew for the first time in 1947 and was claimed to be the first postwar swept-

Derived from the La-150, the Lavochkin La-156 featured a configuration similar to that of Yakovlev's successful Yak-15.

wing jet fighter, but in fact it was used purely for aerodynamic research and never went into production.

The last of Lavochkin's straight-wing designs was the La-174TK, the 'TK' denoting *Tonkii Krylo*, or thin wing. Apart from the wing design, the main difference between this aircraft and the La-152, La-154 and La-156 was that it was powered by an RD-500 (Rolls-Royce Derwent) engine and carried an armament of three NS-23 cannon. The La-174TK, which first flew early in 1948, was in fact something of an anachronism. It contributed nothing to Soviet aeronautical knowledge, except to underline the fact that the straight, thin wing offered no advantages over the swept planform. Before the La-174TK even flew, Lavochkin was already studying two infinitely more advanced jet fighter designs, produced to the same specification as the successful MiG-15. The first of these was the La-168, which was intended to be powered by an RD-10 turbojet. However, when the Lavochkin team discovered that the MiG design, which weighed about the same as their own, was to be fitted with a much more powerful Rolls-Royce Nene engine derivative, they realised that the La-168's chances of success were very slender indeed by comparison. Lavochkin therefore set about building a second prototype, similar in configuration to the La-168 but powered by the production version of the RD-500 Derwent. Somewhat confusingly, this aircraft was given the designation La-174.

The prototype of Lavochkin's La-174 flew first shortly after the La-168 and went on to enter Soviet Air Force service in 1949 as the La-15. However, its performance proved inadequate for the interceptor role. Only a few ground-attack units were equipped with it, the MiG-15 becoming the standard Soviet interceptor of the late 1940s. About 500 La-15s were built.

The first-generation Soviet jet fighters of the 1940s were notable for their ugliness, excessive all-up weight and poor aerodynamic qualities. Nowhere were these shortcomings more apparent than in early Russian attempts to produce a viable all-weather fighter. In 1950, one of the Soviet Air Force's main preoccupations was to bring a true all-weather fighter into service. A specification written around this requirement had been issued two years earlier, and the leading Soviet design bureaux had responded to it; Sukhoi, as we have already seen, produced the Su-15, which broke up in mid-air. The main problem encountered by the designers was that existing power plants were inadequate to compensate for the weight increase that went with the installation of bulky AI radar equipment and the requirement that the proposed fighter had to be a twin-engined machine.

The main contenders in the race to produce a Russian night fighter were Mikoyan, Lavochkin and Yakovlev. Mikoyan's design, the single-seat I-320(R), was powered by two Klimov VK-1 turbojets and first flew in 1949; it was based on the MiG-15, but the engine installation resulted in a bulky, ungainly aircraft with poor handling characteristics and even worse visibility for the pilot, whose forward view was badly obscured by the long nose and radome.

Lavochkin's design, the La-200A, was a better proposition from several points of view, but suffered from the same engine arrangement as the I-320(R). In both cases, the VK-1 engines were fed via a common nose air intake, but in the La-200A they were installed in tandem, the first exhausting under the fuselage and the second under the tail. This necessitated some complex ducting that resulted in an inordinately large fuselage. A central air intake cone housed the La-200A's *Izumrud* radar and the fighter was a two-seater, the pilot and radar observer seated side by side. The La-200A had a fuselage-mounted undercarriage and carried an armament of three 37 mm cannon, which contributed to the high all-up weight of 22,873 lb. Like the I-320(R), the La-200A first flew in 1949, and during trials reached a maximum speed of 660 mph at 16,400 feet; the service ceiling was 59,700 feet.

Neither aircraft underwent extensive operational trials, because in 1950 a developed, lighter version of the *Izumrud* AI radar was successfully installed in a two-seat MiG-15 variant known as the SP-5; both MiG-15s and MiG-17s were subsequently equipped with AI. These variants, however, did not meet the urgent requirement for an all-weather fighter fitted with long-range AI radar, and a specification for such an aircraft was issued in November 1951.

Lavochkin set about modifying the La-200A to carry a new radar scanner in a lengthened fuselage nose. The result was the La-200B, one of the ugliest fighter aircraft ever flown. The massive radome ruled out a single air intake, so the engines were fed by three ducts, one on either side of the nose and one underneath it. Bulky auxiliary fuel tanks were fitted under the wings, and to compensate for the extra weight – the aircraft now weighed 24,750 lb loaded – the undercarriage was strengthened. The La-200B was not the solution to the Soviet Air Force's night fighter deficiency, which was not made good until the deployment of the Yakovlev Yak-25 'Flashlight' in 1955.

Meanwhile, Russian aeronautical scientists had been exploring the realms of high-speed, high-altitude flight with the aid of the DFS

346, a German rocket-powered research vehicle built from technical files captured at the end of the the Second World War. At Podberezhye, the Russians set up a research bureau called OKB-2, directed by a German engineer, Hans Rossing, and A. Y. Bereznyak, the man responsible for the BI-1 target defence interceptor of the Second World War. Most of the personnel were German, former employees of the Siebel company, which was to have built the aircraft at Halle, in Germany.

By the time a second group of German engineers arrived at Podberezhye in October 1946, several models of the DFS 346 were under test, and the full-size aircraft was completed in 1947. The aircraft, which was unpowered, was designated 346P and was designed to perfect landing techniques, gliding in to land after being dropped by its parent aircraft. In all other respects it resembled the intended powered version. The fuselage had an unbroken cigar-shaped profile with mid-mounted wings swept back at 45 degrees and a short, broad fin and rudder unit supporting a swept-back, high-mounted tailplane. The pilot lay in a prone position behind a glazed nose cone.

In 1948 the 346P was transferred to the flight test airfield at Toplistan, near Moscow, where several unpowered, towed flights were made by two German test pilots, Rauschen and Motsch. Powered flights were to be made by another German, Wolfgang Ziese, who had been Siebel's chief test pilot. The powered version of the 346 (it is unclear whether this was a new aircraft, or the original one equipped with a rocket motor) was completed in 1949, the aircraft being designated 346D.

On 30 September 1949, the 346D, with Ziese at the controls, was positioned under the starboard wing of its mother ship, a Boeing B-29 called *Ramp Tramp* (one of three that had made emergency landings in Russia after attacking Japanese targets in Manchuria in 1944). Ziese lit the rocket motor (a Walter HWK-109-509C) a few seconds after the drop and almost imediately experienced control difficulties. Recovering to Toplistan, he touched down at nearly 200 mph on the 346D's landing skid, causing damage to the aircraft and injuring himself.

After the aircraft was repaired, testing resumed at Lukhovitsy airfield in October 1950, the pilot being a Russian, P.I. Kasmin. On 10 May 1951, Wolfgang Ziese, now recovered from his injuries, successfully flew the 346D under power, and on 16 June he made a gliding flight in a second aircraft, designated 346-3. On 13 August 1951 Ziese made a powered flight in the 346-3, somewhat disappointed by the knowledge that in the light of wind tunnel tests the aircraft would never fly supersonically and that it was limited to Mach 0.9.

Ziese made another successful flight on 2 September 1951, but during a third flight on the 14th the aircraft went out of control at 22,000 feet. Ziese had no alternative but to use the 346's novel escape system. The whole nose section was jettisoned by firing explosive attachment bolts and he was pulled clear by the automatic deployment of a parachute.

It was the end of the 346 test programme. In 1953 the German scientists and engineers were repatriated to East Germany. Where, they first heard the news, denied to them during their enforced stay in Russia, that an American research aircraft, the Bell X-1, had flown faster than the speed of sound six years earlier.

CHAPTER FIFTEEN

The X-Craft

I t was bitterly cold in the tiny, cramped cockpit of the little Bell X-1 rocket research aircraft. It was dark, too, for the X-1 was recessed into the bomb bay of the B-29 mother ship, toiling laboriously up the sky to 35,000 feet.

Captain Charles Yeager had been in the cockpit for 45 minutes, his knees pulled up to his chin and his feet level with the seat in a vain attempt to keep warm. His back was against the X-1's liquid oxygen tank, which had a temperature of –140°C, and despite his heated pressure suit the icy cold was slowly eating into his body.

'Chuck' Yeager, aged 24, was one of the United States Air Force's leading test pilots, a member of the small and highly skilled band of men whose task it was to put new combat aircraft through their paces before they were cleared for operational service. Normally based at the USAF Test Flight Division, Wright Field, Dayton, Ohio, Yeager had been transferred to Muroc in California to fly the rocket-propelled X-1, which had been designed by the Bell Aircraft Company for research into transonic flight.

At the end of the Second World War, pushing aircraft to fly at the speed of sound and beyond had been seen as the next major breakthrough in jet aircraft design, but the problems had appeared enormous. German designers had researched the effects of supersonic flight with the aid of high-speed wind tunnels, and aircraft such as the jet-propelled Messerschmitt 262 and rocket-powered Me 163 had flown at high subsonic speeds. However, the handful of pilots who had pushed their aircraft to the edge of the speed of sound had usually not lived to tell the tale, their machines shaken apart by severe compressibility. Mach 1, as the speed of sound was designated under the scale first devised by the Austrian Professor Ernst Mach in 1887, had become a magic number. The

Britain's DH.108 Swallow may have been the first aircraft to break the 'sound barrier', but it cost the life of test pilot Geoffrey de Havilland.

first man to exceed it and survive was assured of a place in aviation history.

In layman's terms, Mach 1 is equal to a speed of 760.98 mph at sea level at a temperature of 15°C, falling to a constant 659.78 mph above 36,098 feet. To probe into these speed realms, joint design studies were begun soon after the war's end by Bell, the NACA and the USAAF, as it then was; the result was the X-1(originally designated XS-1), a sleek, bullet-shaped aircraft with straight, ultra-thin wings and conventional tail surfaces. It was powered by a Reaction Motors bi-fuel rocket motor capable of developing a maximum static thrust of 6000 lb for two and a half minutes.

In the autumn of 1946 the X-1 made its first flight, carried to altitude under a modified B-29 bomber and then released to glide to earth. The first flight under its own power was made over the Muroc Flight Test Base on 9 December. By the time Yeager joined the test programme in the summer of 1947, the X-1 had made several flights. The speed had been pushed up steadily to beyond the 600mph mark, and much information had been assembled on the aircraft's handling characteristics.

Now, on 14 October 1947, Yeager already had eight flights in the X-1 to his credit. The ninth promised to be the most important of all. On this bright, warm California morning, if all went well, he would become the first man in history to fly faster than the speed of sound.

He had risen at 0600 hours, and his wife, Glennis, had prepared a particularly rich breakfast, with lots of eggs, ham and coffee. He would be grateful for it later, in the cold reaches of the stratosphere. Afterwards, he had set off on his usual 30-mile motorcycle ride to Muroc, later to be renamed Edwards Air Force Base. During the journey his thoughts were occupied with many things; not only with the coming flight, but also with a secret that was privy only to Glennis and to a doctor in town. Yeager was nursing a couple of cracked ribs, sustained in a riding accident only the previous evening. Any thought of the risk he was about to take was pushed to the back of his mind.

Only two months earlier, English test pilot Geoffrey de Havilland had been killed when his little swept-wing DH.108 Swallow jet broke apart in a high-speed dive. It was part of the price the British had paid in their bid to be first to exceed Mach 1. They might have succeeded, too, had it not been for a high-level decision by the British Government to suspend work on a highly advanced research aircraft, the Miles E.24/43, or M.52, after the prototype had been half built. It was a decision seen by many as one of the major tragedies of British aviation.

Yeager arrived at Muroc to find the ground crew already hard at work preparing the X-1 and the B-29 mother ship for the flight. On the X-1's nose, the name *Glamorous Glennis* stood out boldly in red, outlined in blue. That had been the idea of Jack Roussel, Yeager's crew chief.

After a lengthy briefing, together with the six-man crew of the B-29 and other personnel who were to be involved in the mission, Yeager put on his pressure suit, parachute, helmet, electrically heated gloves and insulated boots and joined the B-29 crew on board the mother ship. When it reached 7000 feet, he clambered into the cockpit of the X-1 and settled down as best he could to wait for the B-29 to reach launch altitude. During the last few thousand feet he busied himself checking the rows of vital dials and switches in readiness for the drop, looking up from time to time to watch oxygen-masked crew members topping up the X-1's liquid oxygen (lox) tank. This had been filled to capacity before take-off, but lox is an unnatural substance, a gas compressed into a liquid state. If it is not kept under constant pressure, the liquid reverts to a gas rapidly and explosively. Since the lox tended to evaporate quickly during the long climb to height, topping up the tank was a constant task. The liquid oxygen was not the only worry. Behind the lox tank was a second highly volatile fuel, alcohol. A controlled combination of the two would provide the power that would thrust the X-1 to its maximum speed, but any accidental contact between the two fuels during the topping-up procedure would result in an explosion that would destroy both aircraft and their occupants. Yeager said later:

Waiting to be dropped is perhaps the biggest scare. At 1050 the B-29 pilot asked me if I was ready over the radio and I replied 'Yes'. 'Okay,' he said, and then counted. 'Thirty seconds more ... twenty seconds ... ten seconds ... nine ... eight ... seven ... six ... five ... four ... three ... two ... one ... drop!'

I dropped. It felt as though I was on top of a roller coaster. All around me it was bright. It was a few seconds before I could see again. It was like being under tremendous glaring lights.

As soon as I dropped, I began pulling back the control stick to stop the fall. Still falling, I turned on the rocket motor – three of its four tubes. Immediately the plane began climbing. It zoomed up to 42,000 feet in less than a minute. I levelled off and fired the fourth tube. 'I am firing number four now,' I shouted into the mike, 'I am beginning the run.' The plane pulled off at full power. Some of the most thrilling moments in my flying career had come.

The plane accelerated with frightening convulsions. It shook and buffeted terribly for about thirty seconds until I got it up to about Mach One. Then the buffeting left off, but the plane still shook strongly. It was very hard to control, and I had to fly carefully to prevent it turning over. I was too busy to speak into the microphone. Security regulations forbade me, anyway, to tell the others how fast I was going and that men now could fly at supersonic speed.

The Mach needle went higher. I took the speed up to Mach 1.05 and kept it there for about fifteen or twenty seconds. Then I turned off the rocket motor. Not more than two and a half minutes had passed since I had started it. As the plane slowed down the buffeting began again. I jettisoned the remaining fuel overboard; at take-off I had had 600 gallons. Gliding down for about ten minutes, I talked to the people on the ground. I said that it was a very successful flight. I think they understood what I meant. Then we joked about the weather.

All the time two chase planes, F-80 jets, had tried to follow me, but I could not find them any more. Glamorous Glennis had left them far behind. I told the ground crew where I would land and to have the fire trucks there. Landing was easy. The plane stopped rolling, and I turned off the radio and switches. The ground crew helped me remove the door as I got out. I was tired and exhausted and frozen; it felt good to be back on the warm ground of Lake Muroc. There was no ceremony or big congratulating. For all of us this was work, hard work. And security was involved.

'Chuck' Yeager went on to make fifty-three more flights in the X-1, most of them at supersonic speed. On 5 January 1948 he took the aircraft off the ground for the first time under its own power and climbed to 23,000 feet in 1 minute 40 seconds, exceeding the speed of sound in the climb. In February 1948 he pushed the rocket plane past the 1000 mph mark.

Flight at twice the speed of sound now seemed an attainable goal, and in 1950 the Bell X-1 was joined at Muroc by another rocket research aircraft, the Douglas Skyrocket. This sleek, swept-wing aircraft was originally powered by both turbojet and rocket motors, enabling a normal take-off to be made from the ground. Later, the turbojet was deleted and the Skyrocket, now powered solely by a rocket engine, was carried to altitude under a B-29. The man who flew it during this stage of its flight test programme was Bill Bridgeman, a former bomber pilot. Until he joined the Douglas Aircraft Company after a spell as a civil airline pilot he had never flown a jet aircraft. During the Skyrocket's early flights, in which Bridgeman pushed it to the border of the speed of sound, 'Chuck' Yeager often flew as chase pilot in an F-86 Sabre. The Skyrocket went supersonic for the first time on 5 April 1951, after several abortive earlier attempts.

In the early 1950s the quest for higher speeds and greater altitudes gathered momentum. The original Bell X-1, which had taken man to a speed of over 1000 mph, was retired to end its days on permanent display in the National Air Museum of the Smithsonian Institution, but three more aircraft, the X-1A, X-1B and X-1D, were built to continue the research programme. The X-1D was destroyed in August 1951, when it was jettisoned from a Boeing B-50 carrier aircraft over Edwards AFB following an explosion, fortunately without any casualties. Much of the workload now devolved on the X-1A.

Although marred by a number of accidents and setbacks, the NACA piloted rocket programme did not result in loss of life until

The Bell X-1A reached a record speed of 1650 mph in December 1953, with 'Chuck' Yeager at the controls.

1954, and the aircraft involved was another Bell design, the X-2. Unlike the X-1, the X-2 had swept wing and tail surfaces and was designed to reach speeds in the order of 2000 mph. To counter the high temperatures that would be met at such speeds, stainless steel featured predominantly in the aircraft's construction. The X-2 was powered by a Curtiss XLR-25 rocket motor.

Two X-2s were built. Disaster befell the first in May 1954, when an explosion ripped through it as its liquid oxygen tank was being topped up in the belly of the B-50 mother ship. The X-2 pilot and one B-50 crew member were killed, but the B-50 pilot's quick action in jettisoning the rocket aircraft prevented further casualties. The second X-2 made its first powered flight on 18 November 1955, piloted by Lieutenant-Colonel Frank Everest. However, this aircraft was also destroyed in a fatal crash on 27 September 1956, after a flight in which the pilot, Captain Milburn Apt, was officially stated to have flown faster than any other human being.

At that time, the fastest recorded speed was 1650 mph – Mach 2.5 – achieved by 'Chuck' Yeager in the Bell X-1A in December 1953. The launch, from a B-29 at 30,000 feet, was trouble-free. Yeager ignited three of his four rockets, taking the aircraft to 45,000 feet before levelling out and hitting the fourth rocket switch. On this flight the X-1A had 1200 gallons of fuel, enough for four minutes under power. Yeager went supersonic while still in level flight at 45,000 feet, then he pulled back the stick and took the X-1A up to 80,000 feet, exceeding Mach 1.8 on the way up. Levelling out, he pushed all four rockets to full power for the last minute of the flight and watched the needle of the machmeter creep up to 2.5, the aircraft shuddering and vibrating alarmingly. Then, without warning, the X-1A went out of control. Yeager later wrote:

Suddenly the aircraft would not respond to me, It was out of control for about one minute, shooting down from 80,000 to almost 25,000 feet. I was not unconscious, but I was very scared. I wanted to survive. I was doing everything possible to make the plane fly again. I knew I could not get out; the plane had no ejection seat. If I had had time I would have prayed. I was subjected to high forces. My body was aching and my nerves were strained. I had no time to tell the others over the radio what had happened.

I worked like mad. I didn't want to die. Finally, down at 25,000 feet, I regained control of the plane. I went level and glided down slowly to the dry bed of Lake Muroc. The ground crew were there already. They helped me out of my pressure suit. I was sweating and felt exhausted. They took me to the base hospital, where I was X-rayed. Fortunately no bones were broken.

It was Yeager's last flight in the X-1A, as his tour of duty at Wright AFB was over. One of the pilots who took over from him was Joseph Walker, a highly experience member of the NACA test team. On 8 August 1955 he almost came to grief when the liquid oxygen tank exploded as the X-1A was being prepared for a drop from its B-29 carrier. The X-1A had to be jettisoned, Walker being pulled to safety by two B-29 crew members, Jack Moise and Charles Littleton. Their complete disregard for personal safety would later lead them to be awarded the NACA Distinguished Service Medal.

One member of the NACA team in the operations room who had followed the efforts to save the damaged X-1A was a young test pilot named Scott Crossfield, who had also flown the Bell aircraft to more than 1000 mph. Four years later, he was to become the first man to fly a new and far more advanced rocket research aircraft, the North American X-15A.

Following preliminary design studies by the NACA, together with a design competition that encompassed most of the US aircraft industry, in December 1955 North American Aviation was awarded a contract for three prototypes of a manned research aircraft. It was to have a design speed of at least Mach 7 and to be capable of reaching an altitude of at least 264,000 feet, or 50 miles. The power plant was to be a Thiokol XLR-99-RM-1 rocket motor, developing a thrust of 57,600 lb, although initial flight tests with the first two X-15As were made with two Reaction Motors LR-11-RM-5s, each of 8000 lb thrust, as the larger engine was not ready. Because of the intense friction that would be encountered at hypersonic speeds, the X-15A's basic structural materials were titanium and stainless steel. The entire airframe was covered with an 'armoured skin' of nickel alloy steel designed to withstand temperatures of up to 550°C.

The first X-15A flew for the first time on 10 March 1959, carried under the starboard wing of a B-52 Stratofortress. It was not released on that occasion, the first free flight – without power – being made on 8 June, with Scott Crossfield at the controls. On 17 September, with Crossfield once again in the pilot's seat, the X-15A was launched on its first powered flight, dropping from a height of 38,000 feet. The rockets cut in 5000 feet lower down and Crossfield took the aircraft in a shallow climb to Mach 2.3, about 1500 mph. The fuel was exhausted four minutes after the launch and Crossfield came round in a turn to make a dead-stick landing on Lake Muroc, touching down at 150 mph. When the ground crew inspected the X-15A, they found that alcohol from a broken fuel pump had flowed into the after engine bay, causing a fierce and undetected fire, which had burned through a large area of aluminium tubing, fuel lines and valves. It was a sight that, Crossfield later admitted, left him 'sick with disappointment'. Nevertheless, repairs were carried out in twenty-three days and the aircraft was soon ready for its second powered flight.

A number of snags, usually associated with the fuel system, were encountered and had to be solved before the second flight could be made. Eventually, on 17 October 1959, Crossfield and the X-15A were launched from the B-52 at 41,000 feet over the desert. With all eight rocket tubes blazing, the X-15A quickly picked up speed and Crossfield took it in a supersonic climb to 55,000 feet, where he levelled out and made some high-speed manoeuvres before climbing again to 67,000 feet, the maximum altitude for this flight. After the rockets burned out, Crossfield then took the X-15A in a supersonic glide at Mach 1.5, levelling out at 50,000 feet.

At that moment, as the X-15A 'backed' through the sound barrier, Crossfield sensed rather than saw a sudden blur of light flash past his nose – dangerously close. It was Joe Walker, flying an F-104 chase plane. Startled and alarmed, Crossfield radioed: 'There goes my chase, right across my bow!' It had been a near miss – too near. Apart from that one incident, however, the remainder of the flight was uneventful and Crossfield made an excellent landing on the dry lake.

Five days later, Crossfield was airborne in the X-15A once again, with plans to push the speed up to Mach 2.6 at an altitude of 80,000 feet. However, the flight had to be abandoned when he detected a malfunction in his oxygen system, and bad weather delayed further testing until 5 November. This time, the weather was perfect and the pre-flight checks indicated no snags at all. It looked as though the stage was set for a perfect launch.

The countdown reached zero and the X-15A dropped sharply away from its pylon under the B-52's wing. Rapidly, Crossfield's finger flicked over the series of toggles that ignited the aircraft's rocket barrels. They lit up with a thud, and an instant later Crossfield was pressed into his seat by the acceleration as the X-15A began to surge forward under the tremendous power of its motor. Everything seemed to be functioning normally.

Then, without warning, a jarring explosion shook the aircraft. A quarter of a mile behind, test pilot Bob White, flying an F-104 chase plane, noticed a red glare blossom out near the X-15A's rocket exhaust. Anxiously, he radioed: 'Looks like you have an explosion in the rocket motor.' Then, a second later: 'You have a fire!' Acting quickly, Crossfield shut down the engine and jettisoned the tons of fuel that remained on board, informing ground control that he intended to land on the nearest dry lake. The X-15A, still 1000 lb heavier than normal, was descending at more than 300 mph, way above the normal glide speed on the approach to land. Bob White, following the rocket plane down in his F-104, called out the rapidly decreasing altitude. At 6000 feet, Crossfield pointed the X-15A towards Rosamund Dry Lake and levelled out to begin his approach, intent on getting down as quickly as possible. He held the nose of the aircraft high to reduce speed and pressed the microphone button, cutting off any radio transmissions that might interfere with his concentration and distract him during the crucial landing phase.

The ground rushed past in a blur, terrifyingly fast. Seconds later, the X-15A's landing skids hit the surface of the dry lake with a terrific crunch. The nose slammed down and the aircraft ploughed across the desert floor, trailing a vast plume of dust in its wake. Then it slewed to a stop, so abruptly that Crossfield thought the skids had collapsed. The noise died away and he sat there in the cockpit – the safest place in the event of a fire on the ground – and waited for the rescue helicopter to appear. It was on the scene in two minutes. Ground crewmen climbed out and unfastened the X-15A's canopy, helping Crossfield out of the cockpit. Together, they walked around the aircraft and surveyed the damage. It was heartbreaking. The X-15's rocket motor was a burnt-out wreck and the aircraft's back was broken.

After a two-month delay, the research programme resumed with the X-15A-1, which flew for the first time under power on 23 January 1960. Crossfield's damaged X-15A-2 was repaired and flying again early in February, and by October both aircraft had made over twenty successful flights. A third aircraft, the X-15A-3, had been made ready for flight in the summer of 1960, but it was seriously damaged on the ground on 8 June by an explosion in the propellant system. It was several months before it could be made airworthy. This was not the end of the disasters; on 9 November 1962, the X-15A-2 landed without flaps, collapsed its undercarriage and ended on its back, fortunately without serious injury to the pilot.

By this time the X-15s had achieved a number of notable record flights. On 27 June 1962 Joe Walker, now chief test pilot for NASA (National Aeronautics and Space Administration) reached a speed of 4104 mph in the X-15A-1 after the engine burned for 89 seconds instead of the normal 84 seconds. On 17 July 1962 Major Bob White, USAF, climbed to a height of 59.6 miles in the X-15A-3 and qualified for the award of his US Astronaut's 'Wings' by travelling more than 50 miles above the earth. Other pilots who subsequently qualified for a similar award while flying the X-15 were Major Rushworth and Captain J. Engle, USAF, John McKay of NASA and Joe Walker, who on 22 August 1963 set a new record by reaching an altitude of 67.08 miles.

Following its accident in November 1962 the X-15A-2 was almost completely rebuilt and the aircraft was modified to withstand speeds up up to Mach 8. The aircraft flew in its new form on 28 June 1964, when Major Rushworth achieved a speed of 2964 mph at 83,000 feet. On 18 November 1966, the X-15A-2, now fitted with two external tanks designed to improve the burning time from 83 to 150 seconds, reached a speed of 4250mph in level flight at an altitude of 100,000 feet, piloted by Major Pete Knight of the USAF.

That same year, NASA was saddened by the death of Joe Walker, who at that time was probably the world's most experienced supersonic research pilot. On 8 June he was flying an F-104 in close formation with a North American XB-70 Valkyrie supersonic bomber prototype when the two aircraft collided. Both were destroyed. One of the two XB-70 pilots baled out and survived, but the other was killed. Joe Walker's F-104 exploded in flames, leaving him no chance of survival.

By the late 1960s the X-15 was coming to the end of its useful life. One aircraft, the well-tried X-15A-2, had its entire airframe coated with a special ablative material similar to that used to coat the nose cones of missiles. This material was designed to burn away progressively during hypersonic flight, enabling temperatures of up to 1400°C to be withstood. On 3 October 1967, flying this aircraft Major William J. Knight of the USAF reached the highest speed ever attained in an X-15, 4534 mph (Mach 6.72).

The X-15 made its last flight on 24 October 1968, and soon afterwards the programme was suspended. The eyes of America were now on the Apollo lunar landing programme, and the tremendous achievement of the first manned moon landing in 1969 largely eclipsed the efforts of the X-15 team. Yet the contribution made by the X-15A – and, indeed, by the rocket aircraft that had preceded it – to America's space programme was incalculable, particularly in the development of the space shuttle. Perhaps future generations, to whom space travel is routine, might pause to remember Yeager, Bridgeman, Walker, White, Crossfield and all the others who, because it was their chosen career, risked their lives to ride the rockets and make it all a reality.

CHAPTER SIXTEEN

US Combat Aircraft: the Frustrating 'Fifties

Among the large amount of German aeronautical research data that began to reach the USA in the latter part of 1945, were details of some work on tailless designs carried out by Arado. These designs were developed by Chance Vought, leading to the production of the highly unconventional F7U Cutlass. The wing, with a sweepback of 38 degrees, was of very low aspect ratio, 3:1, and almost parallel chord. The pitch and roll controls were combined in elevons on the wing; the fins and rudders were located on the wing at the ends of the centre section.

Although its service career was relatively short-lived, the radical Chance Vought F7U Cutlass had a claim to fame on several counts. It was the first production aircraft to achieve supersonic flight, the first to release bombs at supersonic speed and, in its day, it was the heaviest single-seat carrier fighter in service with any navy. It also set the pattern for future generations of multi-mission combat aircraft, as it was readily adaptable as an interceptor, an air superiority fighter, a low-level attack aircraft or for day and night reconnaissance. But its loss rate was phenomenal. In 55,000 flying hours the Cutlass was involved in 78 accidents (21 of them fatal), resulting in an accident rate of 17 per 10,000 hours, compared with an average for US Navy combat types of 9.81.

The prototype XF7U-1 Cutlass first flew on 29 September 1948 and was followed by a pre-production batch of fourteen F7U-1s for service evaluation, the first of these flying on 1 March 1950. These aircraft were powered by a pair of Westinghouse J34-WE-32 turbojets developing a thrust of 3000 lb (4200 lb with reheat), and with these powerplants the F7U-1's performance fell considerably short of US Navy requirements. The engines provided much less power than was needed to make the F7U safe to fly, much less a potent fighter. Poor engine thrust often resulted in the loss of aircraft. The F7U-1, in fact, was so underpowered that the pilot's manual strictly forbade single engine approaches to carriers. Instead, the emergency instructions called for altitude, if possible, and ejecting, hopefully to safety. The Cutlass was simply too dangerous to risk a single-engine landing.

As serious as the lack of power was, a more serious design deficiency became manifest in the form of a weak drag link brace in the nose landing gear system. The unit frequently cracked during shipboard arrested landings, causing the nose gear to collapse violently. Since the aircraft was designed with a high angle of attack to produce more lift on take-off and landing, its nose dropped about 14 feet when the nose gear collapsed. Almost invariably, the pilot was critically injured or killed.

Chance Vought attempted to remedy the engine power problem by submitting proposals for a version with more powerful engines, the F7U-2, but this was doomed by the US defence cuts of 1949–50. Chance Vought nevertheless persevered with a much redesigned version, the F7U-3, and finally received a development contract in February 1950. Powered initially by two Allison J35-A-21 turbojets, the F7U-3 flew for the first time on 22 December 1951 and completed its carrier trials by July the following year. These trials demonstrated the Cutlass's extraordinary low-speed handling characteristics, vindicating Chance Vought's faith in their tailless configuration. The aircraft also proved to have good manoeuvrability and rate of climb. Nevertheless, it was still underpowered, and the new powerplant that had been selected for it, the Westinghouse J46, was slow to be delivered, with the result that the first F7U-3s did not reach the US Navy's operational squadrons until late in 1954. Even then, the initially promising J46 design proved a disappointment. The J46 design promised 10,000 lb static dry thrust with reheat, but delivered less than half that. In addition, the engines had a relatively short life and needed a great deal of maintenance, with the result that much of the F7U fleet was non-operational for much of its seaborne deployment.

A further problem became apparent when the Cutlass's guns were fired. The aircraft's 20 mm cannon were mounted two on either side, just above the engine air intakes. Both engines had an alarming tendency to flame out when the guns were fired. Initially, the problem was thought to be caused by ingestion of gun gases, but was later proved to be the result of a pressure resonance phenomenon. When both sets of guns fired simultaneously, a pressure wave was created at the engine intakes. This pressure wave caused an organ pipe-type resonance, which then travelled to the aft section of the engine's compressor, creating a stall condition. The resulting air mass led the compressor blades to overheat, perhaps causing the engine to either burn out, or disintegrate. The problem was later solved by installing circuits that prevented the left and right pairs of guns from firing simultaneously, but not before a number of aircraft and pilots were lost simply by firing their weapons at a target.

The first unit to equip with the Cutlass was US Navy Fighter Squadron VF-81, and a dozen other carrier-based squadrons also received the type. Early production F7U-3s were still somewhat underpowered, and most operational Cutlasses were re-engined with the more powerful J46-WE-8A turbojets when they became available. On 12 July 1955, a new Cutlass variant made its appearance; this was the F7U-3M, equipped with launching rails for four Sparrow I beam-riding anti-aircraft missiles and a ventral fuselage pack housing 2.75in Mighty Mouse folding fin aircraft rockets (FFAR). In March 1956, Attack Squadron VA-83, equipped with F7U-3Ms, became the first US Navy missile-armed squadron to deploy overseas, operating from the USS *Intrepid* as part of the US Sixth Fleet in the Mediterranean. Another version, the F7U-3P, also first flew in July 1955; this variant's nose had been lengthened by just over two feet and was equipped with up to five cameras for day and night reconnaissance.

In the attack configuration, the Cutlass could carry an underwing load of up to 5400 lb. By the end of 1958, the F7U had been largely phased out in favour of more advanced types such as the F-8U Crusader, the last operational unit to use it being Attack Squadron VA-66.

Despite all its shortcomings, the Cutlass was popular with most pilots, once they got used to its idiosyncrasies. It was robust and could not be overstressed in high-g combat manoeuvres, and it could out-perform other navy combat aircraft of its era. Perhaps, when everything is taken into consideration, it did not really deserve the derogatory nickname of 'Gutless'.

Another US Navy fighter that remained dangerously underpowered throughout its operational career was the McDonnell

F3H Demon, so much so that it earned itself the nickname 'Lead Sled'. Designed in response to a US Navy requirement for a carrier-based fighter with a performance comparable to that of land-based aircraft, the McDonnell XF3H-1 Demon flew for the first time on 7 August 1951, powered by the new Westinghouse XJ40-WE-6 turbojet, which proved to be extremely unreliable during flight testing. In August 1952, the first prototype was damaged in a landing accident following an in-flight engine failure. Both prototypes were temporarily grounded on two occasions because of engine problems. In addition, early flight testing revealed problems with poor forward visibility, an excessively slow roll rate, and inadequate lateral stability. A redesign of the nose section on production models cured the visibility problem. The roll rate problem was cured by moving the ailerons further inboard, with a corresponding decrease in the length and area of the trailing-edge flaps. The lateral stability was improved by removing the wing fence from each outboard wing panel.

The second prototype was fitted with a 10,500 lb thrust afterburning J40-WE-8 in January 1953. This engine did not prove to be any more reliable than the non-afterburning XJ40-WE-6. This aircraft was used for preliminary evaluation tests at the Naval Air Test Center (NATC) at Patuxent River, Maryland, beginning in

The McDonnell F3H Demon had an unhappy career, mostly because of its unreliable engine.

August 1953. In October 1953, the second XF3H-1 was used for initial carrier trials aboard the USS *Coral Sea* (CVA-43). These trials were fairly successful, but there were some problems with low visibility during carrier approach and landing.

The first XF3H-1 was lost in a crash on 18 March 1954, following an in-flight engine explosion. The second prototype was permanently grounded shortly thereafter. It was later shipped to the Naval Air Development Center at Johnsville, Pennsylvania, to be used in barrier engagement tests.

Meanwhile, the US Navy had decided to place substantial production orders for two variants: the F3H-1N, to be built by McDonnell and powered by a 7500 lb thrust J40-WE-8, and the F3H-3, to be built by Temco and powered by the J40-WE-22. The F3H-1N was powered by the J40-WE-8 throughout its initial trials, but in its production form it was fitted with the J40-WE-22 or -22A engine, rated at 7500 lb thrust dry and 10,900 lb thrust with afterburning. Even with this engine, the F3H-1N was decidedly underpowered, and it was planned to replace the J40-WE-22 with the more powerful J40-WE-24 when it eventually became available.

By September 1953, it was apparent that the J40-WE-24 engine was never going to materialise, and the US Navy would have to be satisfied with the lower-thrust J40-WE-22. The first production F3H-1N took off on its maiden flight on 24 December 1953. The first few F3H-1Ns were intended for service evaluation and carrier suitability tests. In early 1954, the first F3H-1N was turned over for service evaluation at NATC Patuxent River in Maryland.

Production of the F3H-1N proceeded very slowly because of late deliveries of the J40-WE-22 engines. The US Navy service test programme immediately ran into serious trouble. Within the space of only a few days, no fewer than eleven accidents occurred, some of them fatal. Newspaper headlines and editorials screamed about the US Navy having acquired a dangerous and deadly aircraft, one that was more hazardous to its own pilots than to any potential enemy. Not only was the F3H-1N seriously underpowered, its powerplant was prone to in-flight explosions and sudden failures. Consequently, the F3H-1N was a completely unsafe aircraft, and was heartily disliked by its pilots. The problems with the engine proved to be incurable, and the US Navy was forced to call a halt to F3H-1N production after only fifty-eight examples had been built. Work on the F3H-1P photo-reconnaissance variant was stopped before anything could be built, and the contract with Temco was cancelled in its entirety. The US Navy permanently grounded all of its F3H-1Ns in July 1955. The F3H-1N debacle had cost the US Navy some $200 million, most of which had been spent on the unsuccessful J40-WE-22 engine.

The F3H-3 was cancelled altogether. The whole production line was held up until the more reliable Allison J71 turbojet became available, and it was with the J71 that the Demon finally became operational with US Navy Fighter Squadron VF-14 in March 1956. The first Demons to be assigned to the fleet were the F3H-2N night and all-weather fighter variant; further variants were the F3H-2M day fighter, armed with Sparrow missiles, and the F3H-2P photo-reconnaissance aircraft. The first Sparrow-armed F3H-2Ms were deployed with the Seventh Fleet in the Pacific late in 1958, the squadrons in question being VF-64 (USS *Midway*) and VF-193 (USS *Bon Homme Richard*). Twenty-nine of the F3H-2s delivered to the US Navy were in fact F3H-1s, updated and equipped with the J71 engine. One hundred and nineteen F3H-2 Demons were built before production ended in 1959 and the type remained in service until August 1964, the last F3H-3Ms (F-3Bs) retiring from VF-161.

In its efforts to assist the USAF Strategic Air Command (SAC) to build up a potent nuclear strike force in the 1950s, the American aviation industry produced some radical bomber designs, the first of which was the Boeing B-47 Stratojet. All had peculiarities that rendered them dangerous in certain situations, and in the case of the B-47 it was during take-off and landing that the bomber needed extremely careful handling.

The B-47 was a radical departure from conventional design. It featured a thin, flexible wing – based on German wartime research data – with 35 degrees of sweep and equipped with six turbojets in underwing pods, the main undercarriage being housed in the fuselage. It carried underwing fuel tanks, and was fitted with eighteen JATO (jet-assisted take-off) solid fuel rockets to give an emergency take-off thrust of up to 20,000 lb. These were not used during normal operational training, but would have been necessary in a real combat situation to get the B-47, carrying maximum fuel and a 10,000 lb bomb load, off the ground.

The B-47's undercarriage consisted of two pairs of mainwheels mounted in tandem under the fuselage and outrigger wheels under each wing; the main gear folded up into the fuselage, while the outriggers retracted into the inboard engine nacelles. The arrangement was light and space-saving, but gave the B-47 a tendency to roll on take-off, so that in a strong crosswind the pilot had to hold the control column right over to one side. Steering on

The Boeing B-47 Stratojet, seen here in its RB-4H form, was extremely tricky to handle in the landing and take-off phases.

the ground was accomplished by the nosewheel, which was adjusted to prevent the aircraft swinging more than six degrees either way. However, the aircraft's optimum attitude for take-off was the one it assumed as it sat on the ground, and at about 140 knots (depending on its weight), the Stratojet literally flew itself off the runway with no need for backward pressure on the control column. Once off the ground, with flaps up and the aircraft automatically trimmed, the technique was to hold it down until a safe flying speed had been reached and then climb at a shallow angle until 310 knots showed on the airspeed indicator. The rate of climb would then be increased to 4000 or 5000 feet per minute, depending on the aircraft's configuration.

At its operating altitude of around 40,000 feet, the B-47 handled lightly and could easily be trimmed to fly hands-off. The quietness of the cockpit, the lack of vibration and the smoothness of the flight were noticeable, the only exception being when turbulence was encountered at high altitude in jet streams. Then, looking out of the cockpit, the crew could see the B-47's long, flexible wings bending up and down – a rather unnerving phenomenon when experienced for the first time.

The B-47 had a spectacular landing technique that began with a long, straight-in approach from high altitude when the pilot lowered his undercarriage to act as an air brake; with its landing gear down the Stratojet was capable of losing 20,000 feet in four minutes. The flaps were not lowered until the final approach, which started several miles from the end of the runway and demanded great concentration. The bomber could not be allowed to stall, yet its speed had to be kept as low as was safely possible to prevent it from running off the far end of the runway. Each additional knot above the crucial landing speed added another 500 feet to the landing run, so the pilot had to fly to within two knots of the landing speed, which was usually about 130 knots for a light B-47 at the end of a sortie.

Ideally, the Stratojet pilot aimed to touch down on both tandem mainwheel units together, because if only one made contact with the runway first the aircraft bounced back into the air. With the wheels firmly down, the pilot used his ailerons to keep the wings level, much as a glider pilot does after touchdown, and as the ailerons were moved the flaps automatically adjusted their position to help counteract roll; the rudder had to be used very cautiously and sparingly or the aircraft might turn over. To slow the fast-rolling B-47, a brake parachute was deployed immediately on touchdown, and the pilot applied heavy braking. In addition, the aircraft was fitted with an anti-skid device that automatically released the brakes and then reapplied them to give fresh 'bite'. On average, the B-47's landing roll used up 7000 feet (1.3 miles) of runway.

What could happen if a B-47's landing went disastrously wrong was demonstrated on 27 July 1956. A Stratojet went out of control while practising roller landings at RAF Lakenheath, Suffolk, and slid off the runway into the bomb dump. Its fuel tanks exploded, killing the crew, and the resultant fire enveloped a storage igloo containing several nuclear weapons in storage configuration, with no nuclear capsules present. The high-explosive (HE) elements in themselves might have caused a sizeable explosion, but the heat- and blast-resistant nature of the igloo prevented damage to the interior and the HE did not detonate. On another occasion, a B-47 was taking off with one nuclear weapon in strike configuration – in other words, with all components in place, but unarmed – when the aircraft's port rear wheel casing failed at 30 knots. The Stratojet's tail struck the runway and a fuel tank ruptured. The aircraft burned

The long-serving Boeing B-52 had undercarriage problems during its development phase.

for seven hours after crash crews evacuated the area, ten minutes after the accident. The HE element of the weapon did not detonate, but the nuclear capsule was destroyed in the fire and some local contamination resulted.

The B-47 suffered many landing accidents during its career, and never quite lost its reputation as a crew-killer. Its mighty successor, the Boeing B-52 Stratofortress, also had problems in its early stages, although not with such disastrous results. The turbos had a tendency to explode, causing fires or wrecking sections of the fuselage, and the main undercarriage units were a constant source of trouble. On the ground the bomber rested on four twin-wheel units, all of which were steerable and could be slewed in unison to allow crosswind landings to be made with the wings level and the aircraft crabbing diagonally onto the runway; the trouble was that the main gear trucks had a habit of trying to slew in two different directions at the same time, or of jamming in the maximum 20-degree slewed position. The bomber's big Fowler-type flaps also had a tendency to crack and break under the tremendous sonic buffeting set up by full-power take-offs. Problems such as these caused the B-52 fleet to be grounded on several occasions before they were eventually solved, a process that took two years.

One of SAC's biggest headaches, however, was caused by its most revolutionary bomber of the 1950s, the supersonic Convair B-58 Hustler, designed to replace the B-47. The B-58 originated from a 1949 USAF design study competition, which was won by the Fort Worth Division of Convair (General Dynamics). The design was given the designation B-58 in 1951, when Convair was awarded another contract to continue the study of the supersonic bombing concept, and in 1952 a third USAF contract gave the company the go-ahead to produce the B-58 as a viable weapons system. The aircraft was ordered into production in October 1954, and the prototype first flew on 11 November 1956. This was followed by a second prototype and a pre-production batch of eleven YB-58As for testing and evaluation.

The B-58 was a bold departure from conventional design. It had a delta wing with a conical-cambered leading edge, an area-ruled fuselage and four podded General Electric J79-GE-5B turbojets. The three-man crew were seated in tandem cockpits, and the B-58 was the first aircraft in the world in which the crew had individual escape capsules for use at supersonic speed. The aircraft had no internal weapons bay. Instead, it carried a large under-fuselage pod, housing weaponry, fuel, reconnaissance sensors and ECM equipment. Fuel was carried in the pod's lower component, which could be jettisoned under combat conditions when its contents were exhausted. The upper part of the pod was also jettisoned after weapon release, leaving the aircraft aerodynamically clean for the flight out of the target area. The aircraft had a built-in defensive armament of a 20 mm rotary cannon in the extreme tail.

Even before the first B-58s were delivered to SAC's operational squadrons, an alarmingly high accident rate had led to the type's acceptance being delayed by the USAF. The first accident occurred on 16 December 1958, near Cannon AFB, New Mexico, when 58-0018 was lost. The accident was attributed to a loss of control during normal flight when the autotrim and ratio changer were rendered inoperative because of an electrical system failure. On 14 May 1959, 58-1012 was destroyed by fire during a refuelling operation at Carswell AFB. Another aircraft was destroyed on 16 September when a tyre blew during take-off from Carswell AFB, and on 27 October, 55-0669 was destroyed near Hattiesburg, Mississippi, when it lost control during normal flight. On 7 November, 55-0664 was destroyed during a high-speed test flight near Lawton, Oklahoma, when it disintegrated in mid-air, killing Convair test pilot Raymond Fitzgerald and flight engineer Donald A. Siedhof. On 22 April 1960 a failure of the Mach/airspeed/air data system caused the loss of 58-1023 near Hill AFB, Utah, and on 4 June 1960, 55-0667 was lost due to pilot error while flying at supersonic speed near Lubbock, Texas.

The first fully operational B-58A was delivered to the 43rd Bomb Wing at Carswell AFB on 1 August 1960, and in the spring of 1961 the 305th Bomb Wing at Bunker Hill, Indiana, also equipped with the type. The B-58's career was relatively short-lived, the type being phased out in 1969. During that time the Hustler established several international records. However, even one of these attempts ended in tragedy when, on 3 June 1961, B-58 59-2451 crashed after taking off from Le Bourget, Paris, after a record-breaking eastbound transatlantic flight. All three crew were killed.

Of the 116 B-58s built, 26 were destroyed in accidents, mostly during the test and evaluation phase. Others were so badly damaged that they could not be returned to service. It would be twenty years before the USAF received a supersonic strategic bomber on which it could really depend, the Rockwell B-1.

The radical Convair B-58 Hustler suffered a spate of accidents in its early career. Only two SAC bomb wings were equipped with it.

CHAPTER SEVENTEEN

Vertical Flight: the Uphill Path

The story of the vertical take-off and landing (VTOL) application to air combat really begins in 1944, when Germany, as a desperate last-ditch measure, had plans to mass-produce a rocket-powered target defence interceptor known as the Bachem Ba 349 Natter (Viper). Armed with a battery of 73 mm rockets in the nose and powered by a Walter 509 bi-fuel rocket, the diminutive Natter was designed to be launched vertically from

Getting into the Bachem Natter on its launch ramp required considerable contortions on the part of the pilot, as this photograph shows.

a ramp under the power of four auxiliary rocket boosters; the main rocket would then take over and boost the Natter to an altitude of seven and a half miles. After attacking his target, the Natter's pilot would pull a lever, detaching the nose of the aircraft and leaving him exposed to the slipstream; another lever activated a drogue parachute attached to the rear of the Natter, and the sudden deceleration ejected the pilot, who was then supposed to make a normal parachute descent. However, only one manned test flight was carried out, which ended in disaster when the Natter dived into the ground seconds after launch.

Other wartime German VTOL projects, which never flew, were the Focke-Wulf Triebflugel, a jet-powered coleopter (beetle-like) fighter project and the Focke-Achgelis Fa 269 carrier-based fighter that was designed to use thrust vectoring. A single BMW radial engine in the Fa 269's fuselage drove two large-diameter propellers aft of the wing, which could be rotated downwards to provide vertical thrust and rearwards for horizontal flight. The Triebflugel's small jets were mounted at the end of three long arms which, in turn, were mounted at about the mid-section of the fuselage; the idea was that when the arms rotated they would act like a helicopter's rotor blades and lift the device, which sat on its tail.

The main problem confronting designers researching the vertical take-off concept was finding a foolproof means of ensuring stability during the critical transition phase between vertical and horizontal flight. However, in 1951, when the US Navy issued a requirement for a small fighter aircraft capable of operating from platforms on merchant ships for convoy protection, Convair and Lockheed both launched into a research programme that was to produce some surprising results in the long run.

Each company developed an aircraft with a broadly similar configuration, a 'tail-sitter' using a powerful turboprop engine with large contra-rotating propellers to eliminate torque. The idea was that the aircraft, using a simple two-axis auto-stabiliser, would be flown vertically off the ground and then bunted over into horizontal flight. During landing, it would hang on to its propellers, which would then perform the same function as a helicopter's rotor and lower it down to a landing on its tail castors.

The US Navy specification was finalised in 1950, and in March 1951 contracts were issued for the building of two prototypes, the Convair XFY-1 and the Lockheed XFV-1. The latter aircraft was the first to fly, beginning normal flight trials with the aid of a stalky fixed undercarriage in March 1954. For these tests the XFV-1 was fitted with an Allison T40-A-6 turboprop, although plans were in

The Lockheed XFV-1 was never fully evaluated, its test programme ending in 1955.

hand to re-engine it with the more powerful YT-40-A-14 when this powerplant had completed its full series of trials. For vertical take-off and landing the XFV-1 stood on small wheels attached to the tips of its cruciform tail unit, an arrangement that would almost certainly have proved unstable on a pitching deck. The projected armament for the XFV-1 was two 20 mm cannon mounted in wing-tip pods, or forty-eight 2.75 in unguided folding-fin rockets. The XFV-1 made a number of transitional flights before the test programme was concluded in 1955, but its full performance was never evaluated. Performance figures registered during trials,

Convair test pilot 'Skeets' Coleman climbs aboard the Convair XFY-1, which made its first free flight in November 1954.

however, together with wind tunnel data, gave the type an estimated maximum speed of 580 mph at 15,000 feet and an initial climb rate of 10,820 feet per minute.

The Convair XFY-1 was generally a better design. Its flying surfaces were of delta configuration, the wings having a leading edge sweep of 57 degrees. The castor-type undercarriage was also of much wider track than that of the XFV-1, enabling the aircraft to remain stable on its take-off platform at angles of up to 26 degrees from the vertical. It carried 50 gallons more fuel than the XFV-1, and the proposed armament was four 20 mm cannon in wing-tip pods or forty-six 2.75 in rockets. Like the XFV-1, the XFY-1 was fitted with a gimbal-mounted ejection seat that rotated 45 degrees for vertical flight, then slipped into conventional position for flying horizontally. The XFY-1 initially flew in a series of sixty-nine tethered test flights that began in April 1954, with cables attached to the nose and tail allowing the aircraft to rise and descend but limiting lateral movement. The first free flight took place at Brown Field, south of San Diego, in November; the XFY-1 rose slowly to 200 feet, gradually nosed over into a horizontal position, and flew in level flight for twenty minutes. Test pilot J.F. 'Skeets' Coleman then brought it down for a perfect vertical landing. It was the first successful VTOL fighter flight in history, and it brought Coleman the award of the Harman Trophy.

The XFY-1 underwent a much fuller test programme than the XFV-1, achieving a performance that included a maximum speed of 610 mph at 15,000 feet and 592 mph at 35,000 feet. Climbing to 20,000 feet and 30,000 feet took 2.7 and 4.6 minutes respectively, somewhat better than the estimated figure for the XFY-1, and the operational ceiling was 43,700 feet. In 1956, however, the US Navy withdrew its requirement and abandoned the VTOL programme; the reasons given were technical, such as instability during the transitional phase, but the truth was that a powerful lobby of senior officers in the US Navy saw the development of the VTOL concept as a threat to the introduction of newer and larger aircraft carriers. It was to be many years before the VTOL concept returned to the US Navy as an operational reality.

It was the Ryan Aeronautical Company of San Diego that first showed a real interest in the development of pure-jet VTOL, in 1947. The company carried out initial research with an Allison J33 turbojet suspended in a vertical test rig. Later, equipped with a rudimentary cockpit, reaction controls and two-axis auto-stabiliser, this made a series of tethered flights. In 1953, as a consequence of these early experiments, Ryan received a USAF contract to build a prototype VTOL jet aircraft, the X-13 Vertijet. This was intended to be launched from its own self-contained servicing trailer, which incorporated an hydraulically operated inclining launch ramp. The X-13 prototype first flew on 10 December 1955, fitted with a temporary undercarriage for normal take-off and landing trials. Its first vertical take-off was made on 28 May 1956. A second aircraft was built, and this went on to make the full sequence of vertical take-off, transition to horizontal flight and transition back to the vertical for a landing on 11 April 1957. Both aircraft were powered by a Rolls-Royce Avon turbojet, and although they carried just enough fuel for about twelve minutes' flying, they had proved that vertical take-off was a feasible enterprise, provided the engine thrust exceeded the weight of the aircraft by a substantial margin.

Meanwhile, vertical take-off experiments were also progressing in other countries, and they were proving far from trouble-free. In Britain, Rolls-Royce commenced tethered flights of a Thrust Measuring Rig (known more popularly as the 'Flying Bedstead'), which had two Rolls-Royce Nene turbojets installed horizontally at opposite ends of the assembly, their tailpipes directed vertically downwards near the mass centre. In France, SNECMA mounted an Atar turbojet in a special test rig fitted with a four-wheeled undercarriage; after unmanned trials, a piloted version, the Atar Volant, made its first tethered hovering flight on 8 April 1957, followed by a free flight on 14 May. The next step was to enclose the Atar in a fuselage, surrounded by an annular wing to allow the aircraft to change from vertical to horizontal flight; the machine, known as the C-450 Coléoptère, flew for the first time on 17 April 1959, but on 25 July it went out of control as the pilot was trying to stabilise it for a vertical descent. The pilot ejected at 150 feet and was badly injured; the Coléoptère crashed and was totally destroyed. In 1958, the Russians also flew an experimental bedstead-type rig known as the Turbolet, which featured a single vertically mounted turbojet surrounded by a spidery structure and equipped with a fully enclosed cockpit.

Such was the state of the art in 1958. Four countries were involved in VTOL development; one of them, the United States, had already carried out trials with 'tail-sitter' aircraft, and another – Great Britain – was about to start flight testing of a VTOL research aircraft mounted on a conventional tricycle undercarriage. Its name was the Short SC.1.

In 1953, when the Rolls-Royce Thrust measuring Rig was beginning its vertical flight trials, the Ministry of Supply issued Specification ER.143 for a research aircraft which could take off vertically by jet-lift and then accelerate forward into normal cruising flight. Short Brothers' preliminary design, the PD.11 – a small tailless delta aircraft with five RB.108 engines, four for lift and one for forward propulsion – was judged to be the most promising, and in August 1954 Short received a contract to build two prototypes, XG900 and XG905, under the designation SC.1.

The first of these, XG900, was shipped to Boscombe Down in March 1957, and on 2 April test pilot Tom Brooke-Smith took it on its maiden flight, which involved a conventional take-off and landing. XG900 was not fitted with lift engines at this stage, and it was the second Short SC.1, XG905, which began hover trials on 23 May 1958. There followed five months of tethered trials over a raised platform with open-grid decking. The initial free hovers were also made over this platform, but in November 1958 Brooke-Smith landed away from the platform on a football pitch, which was undamaged apart from a slight scorching of the grass. In September 1959 XG905 made its first public appearance at the Farnborough Air Show, where it was intended to demonstrate vertical and horizontal flight; however, the demonstration was cut short in rather embarrassing circumstances when the debris guard over the lift engines' intake became clogged with newly mown grass, causing a sudden power loss that compelled Tom Brooke-Smith to make a rapid descent.

On 6 April 1960 Tom Brooke-Smith achieved the first complete transition from level flight to vertical descent and vertical climb, following a conventional take-off from Bedford in XG905. That summer, XG900 rejoined the test programme, complete with its five RB.108 lift engines. The two aircraft were used to develop rolling take-off techniques from unprepared surfaces, the object being to avoid erosion and also to increase the take-off weight when a short, but not vertical, take-off was permissible.

In April 1961 XG900 was handed over to the RAE at Bedford, while XG905 went back to Belfast to be fitted with a new auto-stabilisation system designed to compensate for gusts. More than eighty flights were made with the new system, starting in June 1963, the development pilot being J.R. Green, who had joined Short from the RAE. On 2 October, Green was returning for a landing when the gyros failed, producing false references that caused the auto-stabiliser to fly the aircraft into the ground. The failure occurred at less than thirty feet, giving Green no time to revert to manual control. XG905 went into the ground upside down, and Green was killed. The aircraft itself was repaired and flew again in 1966, carrying out trials with the Blind Landing Experimental Unit.

At no time was the SC.1 intended to lead to the development of a combat aircraft; indeed, when the SC.1 began its trials in 1958 the Air Ministry showed little or no interest in the concept. The general feeling in Great Britain (and, for that matter, elsewhere) was that the use of four or five engines solely to provide lift would result in a prohibitive weight penalty, effectively cancelling out the combat potential of VTOL.

It was a French engineer, Michel Wibault – whose company had built a range of commercial aircraft during the 1930s – who came up with a possible solution. Wibault envisaged a turbojet using vectored thrust, whereby rotating nozzles could be used to direct exhaust gases either vertically downwards or horizontally aft. Seeking funds to develop his theme, he approached the Paris office of the Mutual Weapons Development Team, which at that time was headed by Colonel Bill Chapman. This was in 1956, at the time when Bristol Siddeley was working on the Orpheus engine to power NATO's lightweight fighter, so Chapman approached Dr Stanley Hooker, Bristol's Technical Director, and sought his views on the Wibault project. Hooker was enthusiastic, and one of his project engineers, Gordon Lewis, was briefed to investigate the possibilities. After preliminary studies, in January 1957 Wibault and Lewis applied for a joint patent covering the design of a vectored-thrust engine known as the BE.52, this was further developed into the BE.53 Pegasus I, which was based on the Orpheus.

In the summer of 1957, details of the proposed engine were passed to Sir Sydney Camm at Hawker Aircraft, who made a preliminary design for an aircraft to go around it. The design was allocated the project number P.1127. It bore no resemblance, at this stage, to the amazing combat aircraft that was ultimately to be developed from it – the Harrier – but it was a firm beginning.

In June 1958, the Mutual Weapons Development Team agreed to pay 75 per cent of the development costs of the Pegasus engine. Funding the airframe, however, proved a tougher obstacle, for research funds had been eaten up by other projects. Hawker had no alternative but to proceed as a private venture while the Air Staff set about drafting an operational requirement to cover the concept. This emerged in April 1959 as GOR345, and Specification ER204D was issued to cover the P.1127, but it was not until October 1959 that Hawker received a preliminary contract for the building of two prototypes. It was fortunate that Hawker recognised potential when they saw it, or there might never have been a Harrier.

In Hawker's opinion, the P.1127 was the ideal design to meet a new NATO requirement, NBMR-3 (NATO Basic Military

The Hawker Siddeley Kestrel FGA.1, developed from the basic P.1127, undergoing evaluation at RAF West Raynham in the early 1960s.

Requirement No. 3, which was issued in 1961 after several revisions and called for a VTOL strike fighter with a sustained capability of Mach 0.92 at low level and supersonic speed at altitude). The P.1127 was not supersonic, but it had a vast amount of development potential ahead of it, and so Sir Sydney Camm proposed a modified version, the P.1150, which was to have a thin wing and an advanced Pegasus engine. Hawker could have progressed with the building of a prototype almost immediately, but yet another revision to NBMR-3, requiring greater range and load-carrying capacity, meant that the P.1150 would have been too small. Camm and his team therefore set about designing a scaled-up version, the P.1154, which was to have a BS.100 engine of 33,000 lb thrust.

However, the P.1154 had a formidable challenger, at least in theory, in the shape of the Dassault Mirage IIIV, whose forerunner, the Balzac VTOL research aircraft, was then under construction. The Balzac used the wings and tail surfaces of the Mirage III-01, married to a fuselage that was completely redesigned except for the main frames and the cockpit section. French research into VTOL, in fact, pre-dated both the Hawker P.1127 and NBMR-3, having been initiated in response to a French Air Force requirement. However, the French chose to pursue their experiments with a combination of lift jets and propulsion engines, rather than vectored thrust. Even then, the engines they chose to power the Balzac were British, consisting of eight lightweight Rolls-Royce RB.108 lift engines and a Bristol Siddeley Orpheus B.Or.3 turbojet for forward propulsion. Ironically, the use of British engines of proven design led to a strong lobby in both the Ministry of Aviation and the RAF that favoured concentrating on the development of the Balzac/Mirage IIIV as the standard NATO strike fighter, at the expense of the P.1154.

The Balzac made its first tethered flight on 12 October 1962 in the rig once used by the ill-fated Coléoptère at Melun-Villaroche, and initial tests were made with a non-retractable landing gear. The aircraft made its first free vertical take-off on 18 October 1962 and the first transition to horizontal flight on 18 March 1963. The test programme continued until 27 January 1964, when the aircraft suffered a critical divergent lateral oscillation during hovering descent. It dropped out of the sky like a falling leaf, crashing and killing its pilot. It was rebuilt, but crashed again on 8 September 1965, killing another pilot. This time it was beyond repair.

Meanwhile, the first flight of the Mirage IIIV had been delayed because of problems in selecting an appropriate propulsion engine. The prototype eventually flew on 12 February 1965, when hovering trials began; at that time the aircraft was fitted with a SNECMA TF-

104 turbofan, but this was subsequently replaced by a more powerful TF-106. The lift engines were eight Rolls-Royce RB.162-1 turbojets. During flight testing, the first prototype Mirage IIIV reached a speed at high altitude of Mach 1.35. The second prototype, which flew for the first time on 22 June 1966, was fitted with a Pratt & Whitney TF-30 turbofan rated at 11,330 lb thrust (18,520 lb with afterburning), and on 12 September the aircraft reached a speed of Mach 2.04. However, it was destroyed in an accident on 28 November, resulting in the cancellation of plans to build further prototypes and develop the aircraft to production standards. In fact, the Mirage IIIV programme had been under critical review for some time, not only on grounds of escalating costs but also because the programme had slipped badly. Originally, it had been expected that the prototype Mirage IIIV would fly late in 1963, and that the first squadron would form in 1966, if trials were successful. Ironically, another Dassault design, the Mirage F, which had been built solely to test the Mirage IIIV's armament system and the TF-306 engine that was to have powered the operational version of the VTOL fighter, was found to have enormous potential in its own right as an operational strike fighter. It eventually entered service as the Mirage F-1, and did everything the Mirage IIIV was expected to do except take off vertically.

In Federal Germany, the design teams of Bölkow, Heinkel and Messerschmitt had joined forces in 1959 at the suggestion of the German Defence Ministry to develop a Mach 2 VTOL interceptor. The design they adopted involved an aircraft of conventional configuration, but with turbojet engines mounted in swivelling wing-tip pods to provide both lift and control in vertical and low-speed flight, together with fuselage-mounted lift engines. A bedstead-type test rig was built and had made 126 flights by April 1965, fitted with a single RB.108 lift engine. The consortium, known as the *Entwicklungsring Süd Arbeitsgemeinschaft*, produced two prototypes of an experimental single-seat VTOL aircraft, the VJ-101C, which were fitted with six RB.145 engines developed jointly by Rolls-Royce and MAN Turbomotoren. Tethered trials of the VJ-101CX-1 began in December 1962, the first free hover being made on 10 April 1963. The aircraft made its first horizontal take-off on 31 August 1963, and its first transition on 20 September 1963. During further trials the following spring the VJ-101CX-1 exceeded Mach 1 in level flight on several occasions, proving the viability of the concept; unfortunately, the aircraft crashed after a normal horizontal take-off on 14 September 1964, the pilot escaping thanks to his Martin-Baker Mk GA7 zero-zero-ejection seat.

Hovering trials of the second prototype, the VJ-101CX-2, began in the spring of 1965, and it made its first free flight on 12 June that year. By this time, Heinkel had dropped out of the consortium, and the resources of Bölkow and Messerschmitt were being channelled into other programmes. Plans to produce an operational version of the VTOL research aircraft, the VJ-101D, were therefore never implemented.

Nevertheless, the two VJ-101Cs had provided a wealth of knowledge about VTOL techniques, and it formed a sound basis for other German companies involved in the field. Foremost among them was the former Focke-Wulf company, which had produced a design study to meet a German Defence Ministry Requirement – VAK 191B – for a subsonic VTOL tactical fighter to replace the Fiat G.91. The initial design study was designated FW 1262, and in 1964 VFW and Fiat agreed to collaborate in development work under a Memorandum of Agreement signed by the German and Italian Defence Ministers. The Italians later dropped out of the programme, but VFW found another partner, Fokker of Holland, and Fiat agreed to carry on as sub-contractor.

Work proceeded with Federal German Government funding, and the first VAK 191B was rolled out in April 1970. It made its first conventional flight on 10 September 1971, and this was followed by a period of tethered hovering trials. By this time the other two prototypes had also joined the test programme, and on 26 October 1972 one of these made the type's first vertical-to-horizontal transition. During this test the aircraft reached a speed of 276 mph, and its RB.126 lift jets were shut down and restarted in flight for the first time. At the end of 1972, however, German Government funding of the VAK 191B was terminated, and no further development was undertaken. By this time, RAF Harriers were being deployed to Germany, and their presence more than adequately filled the V/STOL (vertical/short take-off and landing) requirement in NATO's front line. Hawker's earlier faith had paid dividends, and the Harrier remained Western Europe's only operational V/STOL combat aircraft.

Meanwhile, Soviet experiments with VTOL had resulted in an experimental prototype, the Yakovlev Yak-36, dubbed 'Freehand' by NATO.The Freehand was powered by two non-afterburning Soyuz Tumanskiy/Khatchaturov R-27-300 turbojet engines of 11,000 lb thrust each, mounted forward of and below the cockpit. They were fitted with louvred nozzles, which could be vectored through about 90 degrees and exhausted at the centre of gravity. Engine bleed air was used for reaction control nozzles at each wing-tip fairing, on the tailcone, and at the tip of a ten foot long nose probe. The Yak-36 made its first untethered hover on 9 January 1963. From there, the flight envelope was slowly expanded, with a double transition from vertical take-off to forward flight and back to vertical landing performed on 16 September 1963. The Yak-36 was, in effect, a technology demonstrator that led to the development of the Yak-38 (NATO reporting name 'Forger'), an operational strike aircraft that served on the Soviet Navy's Kiev-class aircraft carriers.

Russia's last venture into the V/STOL field was ambitious, involving the supersonic Yakovlev Yak-41 (NATO reporting name 'Freestyle'). The Yak-41 programme was initiated in 1975, about the same time that the Yak-38 was first being deployed. The supersonic Freestyle was optimised for air defence with an attack capability as a secondary role. The first conventional flight was made on 9 March 1987 and the first hover on 29 December 1989. The first official details were not released by the Soviet Union until the 1991 Paris Air Show, by which time the two flying prototypes, now redesignated Yak-141, had accumulated about 210 hours' flying time. A dozen FAI-recognised Class H. III records for V/STOL were set in April 1991, consisting of altitudes and times to altitudes with loads. During flight testing, the 'Freestyle' achieved a maximum speed of Mach 1.7. Flight testing was originally intended to continue until 1995, but development was stopped in August 1991 because of the shrinking Soviet military budget. Yakovlev funded the development from its own resources for a while, in the hopes of attracting a foreign investor. The second prototype was destroyed after a hard landing on the aircraft carrier *Admiral Gorshkov* on 5 October 1991. The following year, the surviving prototype was demonstrated at the Farnborough Air Show, but the design bureau was still unable to find a market for the design. The Yak-141 was claimed to be as manoeuvrable as the MiG-29, which is doubtful.

The operational use of V/STOL aircraft, by the very nature of the concept, was always going to be dangerous. Between 1961 and 2000 the RAF lost 100 Harriers, including P.1127 and Kestrel development aircraft, to non-combat causes. In addition, the US Marine Corps had lost 143 examples of its versions, the AV-8A and AV-8B, since V/STOL operations began in 1971 and up to 2004. This is a high price to pay for combat versatility. Because of its complexity, the Harrier remains one of aviation history's most unforgiving aircraft, and it will 'bite' the unwary at the slightest pretext. It remains to be seen whether its supersonic successor, the Lockheed Martin F-35, will have gentler habits.

Index